04 MAY 06.

22. JU

13 NOV. 1968
8

23 A

31. DEC. 1969

MAY 19

NOV 2002

29 NOV 1967

(RS

AUTHOR FOX, H. M.	CLASS No. 712·6
TITLE André le Notre:	BOOK No. 86308951

This book must be returned on or before the date shown above
LANCASHIRE COUNTY LIBRARY
COUNTY HALL, PRESTON

LANCASHIRE LIBRARIES

3 0118 06287227 4

ANDRÉ LE NÔTRE

ANDRÉ LE NÔTRE GARDEN ARCHITECT TO KINGS

BY

HELEN M. FOX

B. T. BATSFORD, LTD.

LONDON

Published by B. T. Batsford, Ltd., London

Prepared and produced by Chanticleer Press, New York

Other Books by Helen M. Fox

Patio Gardens
Garden Cinderellas: How to Grow Lilies in the Garden
Gardening With Herbs: For Flavor and Fragrance
Gardening for Good Eating
The Years in My Herb Garden

Translated and Edited

Gardens by Jean C. N. Forestier
The Delectable Garden by Barnard Palissy
Abbé David's Diary: His Journeys in China, 1866–1869

All rights reserved. Except for brief quotations in reviews, no part of this book
may be reproduced without permission from the publishers.
Printed by Brüder Rosenbaum, Vienna.

CONTENTS

		Page
LIST OF ILLUSTRATIONS		6
PREFACE		13
CHAPTER I	Le Nôtre and His Classical Gardens	16
CHAPTER II	The Symbol of an Era	22
CHAPTER III	The Nurture of a Genius	28
CHAPTER IV	Gardens Before André Le Nôtre's Time	38
CHAPTER V	Outstanding Early Work	54
CHAPTER VI	Vaux-le-Vicomte Bursts upon the World	62
CHAPTER VII	Versailles	75
CHAPTER VIII	The Workshop of Versailles	94
CHAPTER IX	Great Projects: Chantilly, Saint-Cloud, and the Terrace at Saint-Germain	110
CHAPTER X	Journeys to England and Italy	123
CHAPTER XI	Old Gardens Remodeled	128
CHAPTER XII	Gardens for the Gentry	147
CHAPTER XIII	Trianon: A New Spirit in the Garden	154
CHAPTER XIV	Old Age with Honors	160
APPENDIX	List of Gardens by Le Nôtre	167
BIBLIOGRAPHY		170

LIST OF ILLUSTRATIONS

	Page
Portrait of Le Nôtre by Carlo Maratta.	Frontispiece
Color map indicating gardens designed by Le Nôtre.	9
Early plan by Le Nôtre of Vic-sur-Aisne (color plate).	10
Later plan by Le Nôtre of Vic-sur-Aisne (color plate).	11
Plan for the gardens of the Château de Pinon (color plate).	12
Statue of Le Nôtre in the park at Chantilly.	25
Bust of Le Nôtre by Coysevox in the Church of St. Roch.	30
Working drawing of grillwork on gate at Versailles.	41
Sketch for palissade at Versailles.	42
Sketch for palissade at Trianon.	43
Sketch of parterre for garden of Monsieur de St. Poange.	44
Drawing from *La theorie et le pratique du jardinage* by Le Blond.	45
Sketch of a parterre from Le Blond.	47
The Tuileries in Le Nôtre's youth.	49
Sketch for Grand Stairway at the Tuileries.	50
Sketch for Grand Stairway at St. Cloud and Luxembourg.	51
The Bishop's Garden at Meaux.	55
The Luxembourg Gardens, from an engraving by Rigaud.	57
Luxembourg Gardens and château.	59
Château de Wideville. View of parterre.	60
The château at Vaux le Vicomte. An engraving by Perelle.	63
Vaux-le-Vicomte. The château.	65
Vaux-le-Vicomte. Grotto and canal. An engraving by Perelle.	66
Vaux-le-Vicomte. Detail of the garden.	71
Vaux-le-Vicomte. View from the château.	72
Versailles. View of the château, gardens and town.	78
Versailles. View of the Orangerie. By Rigaud.	81
Versailles. View of the Orangerie.	83
Versailles. The Fountain of Latona.	85
Versailles illuminated. An engraving by Le Pautre.	86
Versailles. Parterre du Nord as seen from the château.	89

Versailles. The Fountain of Apollo.   91

Louis XIV, Le Nôtre and members of the court making a tour.   93

Versailles. Pageant of *Les Plaisirs de l'Isle Enchantée*.   95

Versailles. Parterre du Sud.   97

Versailles. An engraving by Le Pautre.   99

Versailles. The Fountain of Flora today.   100

Versailles. The Fountain of Les Dômes. Engraving by Rigaud.   104

Versailles. The Fountain of Les Dômes today.   105

The maze at Versailles. An engraving by Le Clerc.   107

Trellis in the maze at Versailles. An engraving by Le Clerc.   107

Chantilly. The great staircase. An engraving by Perelle.   112

Chantilly. An engraving by Perelle.   115

Chantilly. The water parterre today.   116

St. Cloud. An engraving of the gardens.   119

The Tuileries in 1680. An engraving by Perelle.   129

The Tuileries. Plan of the gardens by Le Nôtre.   130

The Tuileries. Bosquet.   134

The Tuileries. Looking toward the Arc de Triomphe.   137

Rambouillet. Parterre.   138

Courances. The gardens as seen from the château.   139

Rambouillet. Showing the quincunx layout of trees.   140

Rambouillet. An engraving by Rigaud.   143

Château de Maintenon. The moat.   145

Maintenon. View of the unfinished aqueduct.   146

Clagny. A plan of the gardens.   150

Trianon. An engraving by Rigaud.   156

Pontchartrain. Plan for the gardens.   161

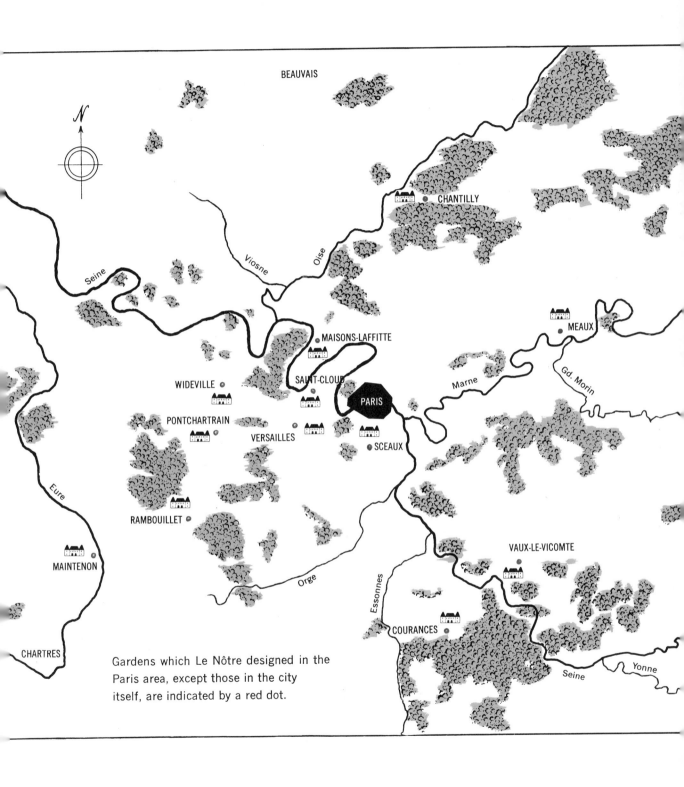

BEAUVAIS

N

Viosne

Oise

Seine

CHANTILLY

MEAUX

MAISONS-LAFFITTE

Gd. Morin

WIDEVILLE

SAINT-CLOUD

Marne

PARIS

PONTCHARTRAIN

VERSAILLES

SCEAUX

Eure

VAUX-LE-VICOMTE

RAMBOUILLET

Orge

Essonnes

MAINTENON

COURANCES

CHARTRES

Seine

Yonne

Gardens which Le Nôtre designed in the
Paris area, except those in the city
itself, are indicated by a red dot.

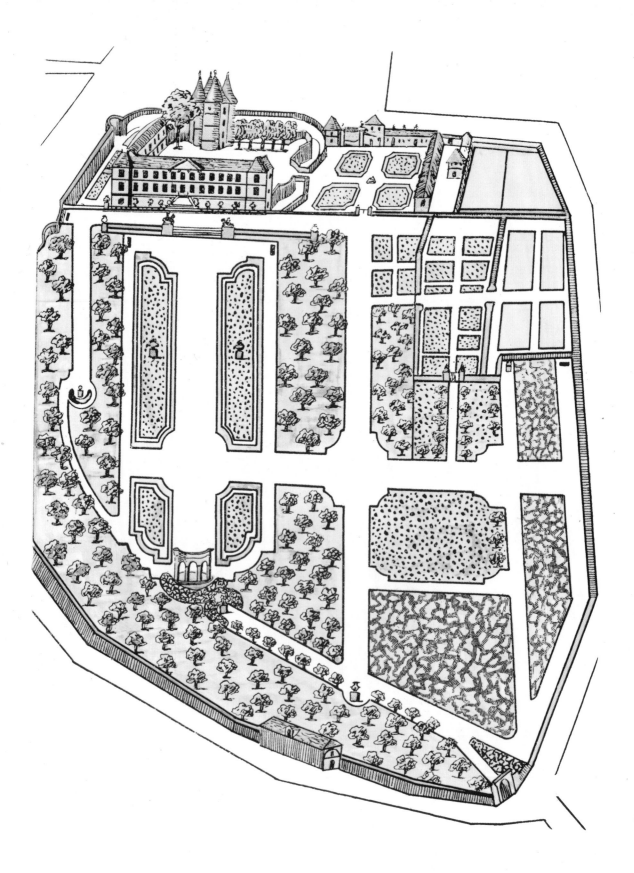

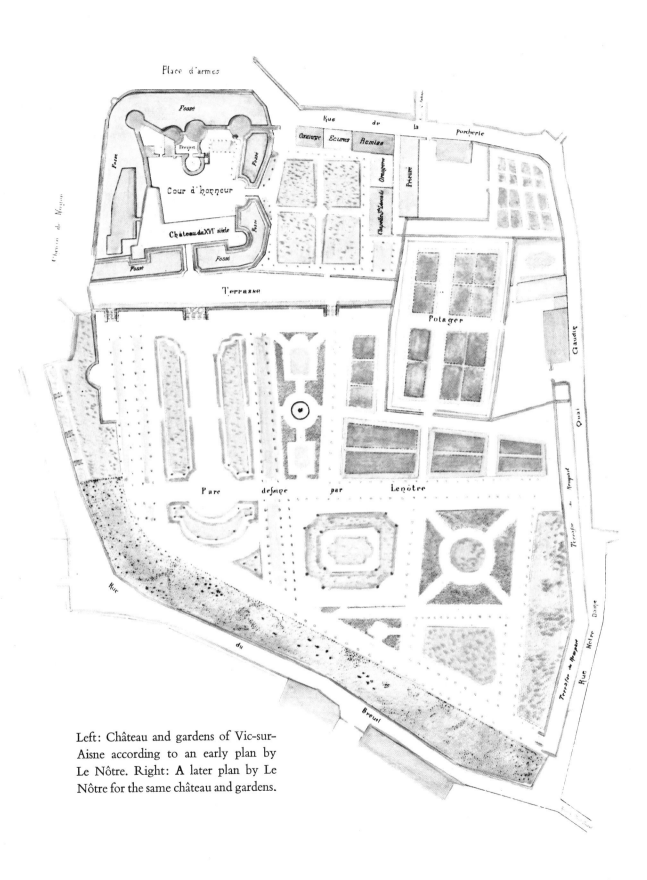

Left: Château and gardens of Vic-sur-Aisne according to an early plan by Le Nôtre. Right: A later plan by Le Nôtre for the same château and gardens.

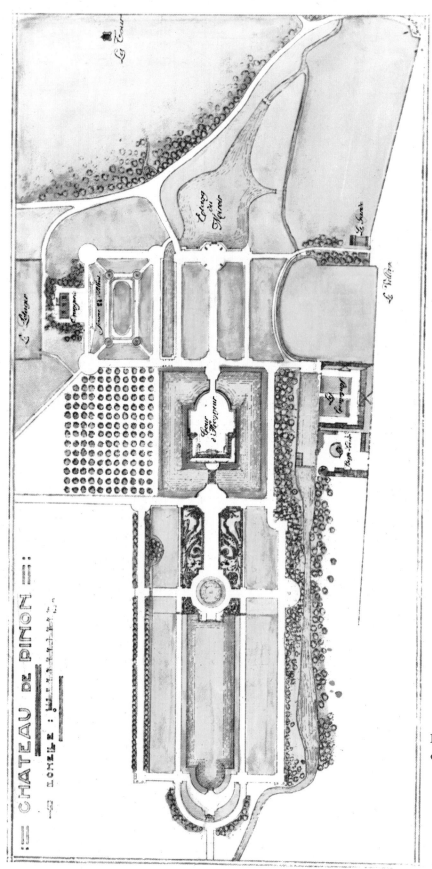

Le Nôtre's plan for the gardens
of the Château de Pinon.

PREFACE

One spring in Paris I was walking across the rue Royale and into the Tuileries with Jean C. N. Forestier, curator of parks and gardens of the city, an outstanding landscape architect, and the author of a book, *Gardens*, which I had translated. When we came to the place where the statue of Jules Ferry now stands, Monsieur Forestier said, "This is where André Le Nôtre had his house."

Though I had made many visits to France and as a little girl had gone to school there at a convent in Saint-Germain-en-Laye, I knew very little about Le Nôtre. So I asked Monsieur Forestier to tell me about him. Le Nôtre was his hero for he had been the greatest landscape gardener in France if not in Europe. Moreover, Monsieur Forestier was the proud possessor of some books and engravings that had belonged to Le Nôtre. There in one of the beautiful gardens which Le Nôtre had recreated and which were now under Forestier's care he told me the story of the great gardener of the 17th century, of his winning personality, his genius and what he had meant to France. Without realizing what I was undertaking I said, "I would like to write the story of his life and gardens."

I soon found that a work of this kind needs thorough preparation. I had a foundation for this, having studied landscape architecture for two years with Harold Caparn and having been a gardener all my adult life. But I nevertheless devoted my spare time during the ensuing fifteen years to learning about seventeenth century France and in visiting Le Nôtre gardens wherever he was said to have had a hand in the design, in France, Italy and England. Many hours were spent in the New York Public Library and some time at the Metropolitan Museum of Art, where I studied the prints of the era, and the furniture and paintings as well. At the Columbia School of Architecture I took a course in baroque architecture under Professor Hudnut, then dean of the school; there also I read in the excellent library. One summer in France, while my children went to school in Tours, I pored over illuminated manuscripts delineating oldtime gardens.

One of the most delightful experiences in my preparation was another summer spent in Paris and Versailles, investigating original sources and studying, on the spot, gardens designed by Le Nôtre or remodeled by him, as well as gardens of architects who had preceded him.

On this Paris visit I was fortunate to have a curator from the Louvre, Madame Oberlander, accompany me and open doors of libraries and museums so I could see old prints and books without having to waste too much time with red tape. Through her I was able to examine some of the material which had been assembled for the exhibition held at the Louvre celebrating the three-hundredth anniversary of the birth of Le Nôtre. At Versailles, where I went to be near the library and the park, I lived in a house that had belonged to Vatel, maître d'hôtel of Fouquet and later of the Prince de Condé. This elegant house, which had been turned into a hotel, made clear how influential and wealthy were the upper servants of seventeenth century nobility.

Everyone I met in France was most helpful and pleased to find me studying Le Nôtre, from conductors in railway trains (one of whom said, "*Le Nôtre était un bon jardinier*") to concierges in hotels and owners of bookshops. The most valuable books I came across were Jules Guiffrey's *André Le Nôtre* and Lucien Corpechot's *Les jardins de l'intelligence*, the only ones devoted entirely to Le Nôtre. The owner of the delightful garden of Pomponne told her gardener to be sure to turn on the waters before I went into the garden so I would get the right effect. One day I hired a car to go to Vaux-le-Vicomte, formerly the estate of Fouquet; when I went to pay for the car, the owner of the garage asked me how I had liked Vaux, which he had never seen. I told him it was like a dream come true. Then, leaning on the gas pump, his hands oily from work, he asked me, "Who do you think was right, Madame, Louis Quatorze or Fouquet?"

In the library of the town of Versailles, which had formerly housed the Foreign Office, the librarian showed me the room where the French minister of foreign affairs had signed the treaty recognizing the independence of the American Colonies. When I commented on the elegance of the walnut bookcases festooned with carved wreaths of flowers, he said the library had belonged to the Marquise de Pompadour. He introduced me to a rosy-cheeked old gentleman with a white goatee who came to the library almost every afternoon with a pretty young secretary to engage in research. The old man specialized in studying the streets of Versailles and wrote informative articles on them in the *Revue de Versailles*—where I also found material on the house owned by Le Nôtre. In the palace, now the Museum of Versailles, Monsieur Brière, who had succeeded Pierre de Nolhac as Curator, was helpful too. He let me go into rooms at hours before and after tourists came, so that I might study furniture and paintings, and told me about the material on Nicodème Tessin's visit.

It took me a long time to digest and organize all the material I had gathered and of course I had far more than I could use. But at last I felt I had been able to reduce it to a form useful to present-day readers. I am convinced the ideas presented in this book are needed for a better understanding in planning of parks and gardens; that Le Nôtre's classical gardens, though often condemned as too stiff, are masterpieces of landscape architecture; that their basic principles of garden design can be adapted with great advantage even to the simplest backyard as well as to vast housing developments and city-planning schemes.

I hope that this book will make Le Nôtre better known and appreciated by the English-reading public. It has, perhaps, few thrills, except for those who can share my own joy in my discoveries about him, and for the many to whom it may introduce ideas about park and garden design. His story is that of a serious, hard-working genius, who left us few words, but many ideas which we still can see demonstrated in places he made beautiful.

Recently, a bust of Le Nôtre, a replica of the one in the Church of St. Roch on the rue Honoré, has been put on the platform above the steps leading out of the Tuileries, near the Orangerie. From there one can look up the vista of the Champs-Elysées created by Le Nôtre. A plaque under the bust bears this legend: "*André Le Nôtre, auteur de ce Jardin, de ceux de Versailles, Chantilly, Saint-Cloud, Meudon et les plus beaux parcs de France. 1613–1700.*"

Mount Kisco, 1962.

CHAPTER I

LE NÔTRE AND HIS CLASSICAL GARDENS

ANDRÉ LE NÔTRE was one of the supreme artists of the seventeenth century in France. It was he who perfected the classical style of gardening which had grown from Mediterranean roots and developed slowly through the centuries. Outstanding among his works are the park-like gardens of Versailles, Vaux-le-Vicomte, Saint-Cloud and Chantilly. He remade the park of the Tuileries, remodeled portions of the park at Fontainebleau, and made over the parterre at Saint-Germain where he was the architect of the great terrace overlooking the Seine.

In Paris he drew the broad avenue of the Champs Élysées from the Tuileries through the walls of the city straight out across what were then uncultivated fields to the site of the present Arc de Triomphe. This arch is now the center of a star made of radiating avenues—which are in themselves similar to roads in his parks. Indeed, parts of Paris, with buildings set amid parterres, vistas, groves of trees and open squares bright with flowers, are, so to speak, Le Nôtre parks, urbanized. Besides great parks, Le Nôtre designed hundreds of gardens, many of them for private owners throughout France and even a few in Germany, Italy, Belgium and England.

During the French Revolution, almost two hundred years after the death of Le Nôtre, his tomb was opened and his bones scattered, because the people recalled that he had been closely associated with Louis XIV and the royal expenditures at Versailles. For years the work of Le Nôtre had been belittled, much of it being either credited to others or regarded as of unknown authorship. Under the Republic and with the adoption of a fresh view of history, the French recognized and appreciated the benefits conferred on France by the Valois and Bourbon kings. It was then that they reconstructed some of their palaces and restored the parks.

When at last the French began to study the records of André Le Nôtre, they appreciated his greatness as a designer of gardens and came to love his personality. In the gallery at Versailles where portraits of artists, writers, architects and statesmen who made the reign of Louis XIV the most brilliant period in French history have been assembled, there is a painting of Le Nôtre (executed in Rome by Carlo Maratta) when he was sixty-three years old. After Le Nôtre's return to France, Antoine Coysevox, celebrated contemporary French sculptor, who was closely associated with Le Nôtre, made a portrait bust of him standing in the Chapel of Saint-André; Le Nôtre gave this chapel, where he was married and buried, to the Church of Saint-Roch in the rue Saint-Honoré.

These portraits show Le Nôtre as handsome, lively, and forceful-looking. In the painting he is dressed in the ornate fashion of the day. He wears a brown wig with curls descending to his shoulders. Below a jabot of fine lace hangs the blue ribbon of the order of Saint-Michel which was given to him after the order of Saint-Lazare and was tantamount to ennoblement. His complexion is ruddy from living out-of-doors; his light blue eyes have an expression of surprise and mockery; the nose is aquiline, the lips wide and sensuous yet pursed with determination, the chin tending to be double but nonetheless strong. His whole person expresses power and self-mastery. The hands, as with many artists, have long fingers square across the tips. In the Maratta portrait he is shown holding a plan in one hand and extending the other as if pointing to some project.

Descriptions of Le Nôtre by his literary contemporaries characterize him as vivacious, exuberant and enthusiastic. He spoke and wrote in the chaffing style, with a touch of cynicism that had been made fashionable at Versailles by Madame de Montespan. To this day his witty sayings are repeated and have become part of French legend. So has the story of his career, that of a gardener who, beginning with spade and hoe, developed his abilities until he designed the finest parks in Europe, acquired great wealth, had one of the best art collections in France, and became the close friend of

Louis XIV, all without ever belittling or forgetting his origin or his place in the social hierarchy. To the French, who excel in farming and gardening, Le Nôtre because of his amiable character is known as *le bon jardinier* and in consideration of his achievements they speak of him as "Gardener of Kings and King of Gardeners."

Le Nôtre was the third generation of his family to become a royal gardener. He grew up in close association with the royal family, members of the court, and the artists and artisans employed by them. He was conspicuous at court as an independent and forthright person in contrast to the men and women who sought only the King's patronage. Louis XIV liked him and enjoyed his company; he was amused at Le Nôtre's wit, enthusiasm and bursts of affection. Moreover, the King appreciated the gardener's taste and ability and showered him with emoluments.

Le Nôtre had innate tact and an exceptional understanding of people. He seems never to have antagonized anyone nor to have aroused jealousy, as well he might, not only because of his closeness to the King but also because of his superlative talents; on the contrary he was liked and favored by all. Courtiers and artists, mistresses and ministers rose and fell, yet Le Nôtre retained the King's favor and affection to the end. Madame de Montespan had him design her garden and so also did her rival and successor, Madame de Maintenon. He worked for Colbert and designed his park at Sceaux. After the minister's death, when his enemy Louvois succeeded him, Le Nôtre made over his garden at Meudon.

When the King was at Versailles, on the days when he did not hunt, he would make a tour of the park according to an itinerary he himself had devised. Le Nôtre would be close beside him; flanking and following after them would be nobles, architects, artists and visitors of note, sometimes as many as a hundred in all. Once when they paused to look at the *Bosquet des Trois Fontaines*, then under construction, the King suggested some changes. Turning to Le Nôtre he added, "In appreciation of your fine work in all the royal parks we are going to bestow upon you the order of Saint-Lazare. And tell us what you are going to take as a coat of arms?" Le Nôtre stopped to think, pursing his lips while King and court waited for the anticipated witty reply. Then, his eyes twinkling, he answered, "Three snails and a head of cabbage—but I must not forget my spade for it is due to my spade that I am the recipient of all the kindnesses with which Your Majesty honors me."

Le Nôtre and the King shared the ambition to beautify France and glorify the reign. They also shared a deep interest in art and both were keen collectors of specimens in a wide range of fields. They were especially interested in medals and would examine them together bending their heads over them while discussing some rare specimen of the famous collection which Le Nôtre kept in his house in the Tuileries gardens.

It may seem odd to include an obituary of the hero in the introductory chapter but the opinion expressed by the Duc de Saint-Simon at Le Nôtre's death sums up so well what his contemporaries thought about him that it may well be used to set the tone for this book. The pen portraits scattered throughout the duc's celebrated memoirs are often tinctured with malice, for he was disappointed at not receiving the recognition he thought he deserved. But in writing about Le Nôtre he had only praise:

> *Le Nôtre died about this time, being eighty-eight years old, in perfect health and with all his faculties and good taste intact to the very last. He was illustrious as having been the leading designer of those beautiful gardens which adorn France and which indeed have so much surpassed the gardens of Italy that the famous masters of that country come here to admire and learn. Le Nôtre had a probity, exactitude, and uprightness which made him esteemed and loved by everybody. He never forgot his position and was always perfectly disinterested. He worked for private people as for the King with the same application—seeking only to aid nature and to attain the beautiful by the shortest road. He was of charming simplicity and truthfulness—the King liked to see him and talk to him.*

When the visitor stands on the terrace in front of the château at Versailles and looks at the vast landscape before him, his eyes follow along the central vista that leads over pools and lawns and continues seemingly into infinity. He notices how this main axis, as a result of perspective, seems to rise to meet the horizon. The impression is so stupendous that he invariably feels insignificant. He may well feel insignificant, for here he is raised above the trivial everyday life and faced with the calm of a major achievement.

The work of André Le Nôtre represents the apogee of classical garden design, a style also called French, architectural or formal. In the United

States we are not familiar with gardens of French origin because in the art of garden design, as in literature, we have followed English ways of expression. The majority of American gardens are laid out in a style variously called English, romantic or naturalistic.

The classical garden took form in an age when man imposed precise patterns of his own making on mankind as well as on the landscape, whereas the romantic garden came into existence after the idea of freedom for the individual had been accepted, after nature was enjoyed and plants as well as human beings were encouraged to express the qualities inherent in them.

Italy and Spain, and also Persia, each developed its own form of classical garden by combining Greek, Egyptian or Roman sources with their own traditions and needs. The designers of French classical gardens merged their own medieval patterns with the Roman. Down through the centuries as the political framework of the country grew more unified politically so too the literature, architecture and the gardens developed greater unity.

By Le Nôtre's time house and garden were indivisible and complemented each other. Generally the garden began with a broad terrace which was part of the house while its main axis flowed out from the principal doorway and often had a series of room-like enclosures on either side of its length. Ponds and fountains were planned to be on axis with windows so as to be seen from certain rooms. Like the house, the outlines of the garden were geometrical and the plan either symmetrical or balanced. There was no intention of imitating nature; on the contrary, architectural features such as pavilions, stairways, balustrades and statues were considered the most important ornaments in the gardens, and living plants were treated as subsidiary furniture. Shrubs were pruned to follow geometric shapes, and flowers were trimmed to provide lines or sections of color in patterns similar to those in tapestries, embroideries or rugs. Streams were made to flow between stones or tiled banks while the outlines of ponds were carried out from designs first drawn on paper with a ruler and compass.

There were unities in garden design similar to the unities of classical Greek and contemporary French drama: unity of time as brought about by the harmony between house and garden; of place, in the way each part contributed to the whole; and of action, by the concentration of interest in the garden through the exclusion of all views of meadows and valleys and the constantly changing traffic along roads. This last was accomplished by high walls and by groves of rigid trees planted closely together or by skillful grading of the land.

However, the architectural garden is not new or unknown in the United States. There are many private gardens in the French tradition, such as the famous Middleton Gardens on the Ashley River in South Carolina, and public gardens, such as the mall and the steps and fountains at the lake in Central Park and Bryant Park in New York City, the lakeside in Chicago, and Jones Beach State Park in Long Island. Pennsylvania Avenue with the vista from the Capitol to the White House in Washington, originally planned by Pierre Charles L'Enfant at the end of the eighteenth century, is also in the French tradition.

Today, when man is trying to keep his personal freedom in the face of new limitations, is a good time to re-examine the classical gardens of Le Nôtre. The garden of the future might well adapt ideas, gleaned from these, to meet new requirements. Moreover, so much has been written about the romantic garden that an account of the classical style and the story of its greatest exponent, André Le Nôtre, would seem to be timely.

CHAPTER II

THE SYMBOL
OF AN ERA

THE CLASSICAL GARDENS of André Le Nôtre, with their parts related by mathematical formulas and with an infinite variety of details held in restraint to obtain clarity and unity, express the political and philosophical thoughts of seventeenth century France. Therefore though this is primarily a garden book, it may be helpful to review briefly the political background of the period in which Le Nôtre lived.

In 1609, four years before Le Nôtre was born, Henry IV was assassinated. He had strengthened the monarchy by accelerating the liquidation of feudal lords whose rivalries caused civil wars, division of power, and disorder. After he died, the process of unification continued through Richelieu, who ruled on behalf of the widow Marie de Medici, mother of Louis XIII.

After Richelieu died, Mazarin ruled France for the Spanish princess, Anne of Austria, who was regent for her son, young Louis XIV. It was during Mazarin's sway that the "nobles of the pen" became prominent; it was they who built superb houses and laid out magnificent parks in which Le Nôtre had a hand. Among them were René de Longueil, president of Parliament, who built Maisons, Jacques Bordier who built a house at Raincy, Seguier at Meudon, and Claude de Bouillon in Paris and at Wideville. But the "nobles of the sword" continued to agitate. During their last uprising, called the Fronde, which lasted from 1648 to 1653, the mob became so menacing that the young King with his mother and brother were aroused in the night by their anxious relative, the Prince de Condé, and driven secretly from the Tuileries to Saint-Germain.

The memories of this experience were never to grow dim for Louis. He never forgot what it was like not to have enough to eat, to live in unfurnished and unheated rooms, and to be hard pressed for money. Nor did he forgive those who sided against him. The memory caused him to spend fabulous sums on the embellishment of his country estates in preference to his residences in Paris. At Versailles, in the center of the parterre below the great terrace in the heart of the park stood a sculptured group representing Latona being reviled by peasants whom Jupiter, in response to her entreaties, is turning into frogs. This was widely accepted as a rebuke to the nobles for their revolt during the Fronde.

Louis' influence on art was in the direction of measure and balance. He had a keen sense of proportion and a correct eye and was able to detect at a glance the slightest deviation in a line or angle. His influence on manners was to make them highly formal. Dr. Martin Lister, an English doctor who kept a diary of his visit to France at the end of the century, wrote: "Monsieur Le Nôtre spoke of the good humor of his master; he affirmed to me he had never seen him in a passion and there have been many instances and occasions that would have caused most men to have raged: which yet he put by with all the good temper imaginable."

Louis loved his job of being king, was determined to excel, and worked hard at it for seven hours a day or longer. He believed he ruled by the will of God, and he thought of his subjects as chattels to be used as he wished yet he had perfect manners and dignity of bearing. It should of course be pointed out that except for Vincent de Paul, who was helping to alleviate appalling conditions in hospitals and orphan asylums, aided by a group of charitably-minded aristocrats, almost no one at that time considered serfs or peasants as human beings or deserving of any consideration. Le Nôtre himself gave generously to funds for the starving during periods of famine when crops failed and conditions were so dreadful that something had to be done about it, if only temporarily.

After Mazarin's death and Fouquet's disgrace, Jean Baptiste Colbert was promoted to be first minister. Everywhere he went thereafter, he carried under his arm a black silk briefcase containing close accounts of the vast sums being disbursed, often against his judgment. For though he sympathized with the king in wanting France to shine, he also desired a balanced budget. The two men, both efficient executives, bureaucratized each branch of the government so meticulously that in time the various departments composed as unified a whole as the terraces, fountains, views and forests of a Le Nôtre park.

Important in the unification of France was the building of roads. They served strategic purposes, leading from one citadel to the next; but they also encouraged commerce. As far as Le Nôtre was concerned, they enabled him to travel in his coach instead of on horseback when he visited the gardens he was designing in all parts of France, and even in Germany and Belgium, or when he traveled in his capacity as *contrôleur de bâtiments*.

At this time, too, the army was transformed from a feudal into a modern organization; and a navy was created and expeditions sent to colonize distant lands. Home industries were also encouraged. Under Louis, with Colbert to supervise and direct, a school was established at the Gobelins where French artists and artisans were taught to weave tapestries, to carve in wood and stone, make statues and paint; in other schools students were taught to make laces and weave silks, often by teachers imported from Italy and Belgium.

In Louis' reign the arts flourished as only once before in France, namely during the eleventh and twelfth centuries, when the great cathedrals and abbeys were built, when Abelard taught at the university in Paris, and Abbé Suger was director of the Monastery of St. Denis. Louis made of France a work of art and the people a nation of artists and skilled artisans.

In those days men thought that mathematics could provide the key to understanding ideas. At the beginning of the century logarithms and infinitesimal calculus had been discovered and Descartes was the first to use mathematical shorthand for a variety of purposes instead of only for certain experiments. Pierre de Fermat and Blaise Pascal made other important mathematical discoveries and it was Descartes who crumbled the last medieval defenses barring the way to independent thinking when he declared, "I think, therefore I am." He further cleared the way for scientific experiments when he decided "never to accept anything for true which I did not clearly know to

Statue of Le Nôtre in the park at Chantilly.

be such; that is to say, carefully to avoid precipitancy and prejudice and to compromise nothing more in my judgment than what was presented to my mind, so clearly and distinctly as to exclude all ground of doubt.''* Pascal, too, would believe only what had been proven clearly and decisively.

The new methods of calculation led to a clearer understanding of natural phenomena and also enabled architects and engineers to build complicated waterworks and to plan terraces and grading as well as houses with an accuracy not heretofore possible. Le Nôtre made use of the new discoveries to produce optical illusions with water and grading, notably at Vaux, Chantilly, and Versailles.

In the forties and fifties of the seventeenth century men and women gathered in the Duchesse de Rambouillet's famous "blue salon" to read aloud their plays and essays and discuss rules of grammar and literary expression. Such salons, and others held later at Madame de Sevigné's and the Maréchale d'Albret's, and lastly those at the court itself under Mesdames de Montespan and de Maintenon, refined manners, gave conversation, then regarded as an art, its wit and verve, and imparted to writing an admirable clarity and restraint. From the salons issued schemes for academies of literature, painting and sculpture, also of science and architecture, where artists could meet and exchange ideas. Some of the academies were consulted on royal building projects.

During the time of Le Nôtre the artists who embraced new ideas were called "modernists," and those who opposed change, "classicists." The dispute between the two schools was carried on with asperity but with elegance. Admiration for antiquities was strong; and artists were constantly sent to Rome to copy and buy antiques for royal estates.

The cause for the modernists was championed by Charles Perrault when in 1687, at the French Academy of Literature, he read a poem entitled *Le siècle de Louis le Grand* in defense of his ideas wherein he expressed the growing confidence of French artists. He agreed wholly with Descartes' statement: "We have no reason whatever to respect the ancients because of their antiquity. It is we who are the ancients for the world is older today than in their time and we have had more experience."

Le Nôtre was of the same opinion as Perrault and encouraged

* *Discourse on Method.* Translated by John Veitch. Everyman's Library.

living artists by bringing them to the King's notice and buying their work. Thus, early in the reign, French artists, with Le Nôtre, balked the famous Italian architect and sculptor Bernini from carrying out his design for the Louvre for which he had been brought to France. Behind the scene, they were working for Le Vau and against Bernini, despite the fact that the latter was far more experienced.

Long before Le Nôtre, the religion, philosophy and way of life of a people had been expressed in the form of a garden in China and Japan, and again in Persia and India. This had occurred in Italy, too, and was to happen again in England. In each of these countries many artists designed the gardens. But in France it was only one artist, André Le Nôtre, who expressed the civilization of his time through the medium of his work, and did it so vividly, aptly and brilliantly that his gardens are the perfect symbol of his era.

CHAPTER III

THE NURTURE
OF A GENIUS

INSIDE THE palaces, kings and nobles were intriguing for power; along the boundaries of France fighting was in progress; but in the royal gardens, Jean Le Nôtre, father of André, and his associates peacefully pursued their tasks year in and year out according to the seasons. Their day's work is described by Jean de La Quintinie in his book *Instructions pour les jardins fruitiers et potagers*. In January they forced hyacinths and tulips in hotbeds for early spring bloom; after these had been taken out and planted in the beds, seeds of annuals, such as carnations, stocks and calendulas, were sown and transplanted to the garden to follow the bulbous plants. The heavy work of spring consisted in hardening off exotics and bringing them from their winter quarters in the orangerie, a sun-heated building with large glass windows facing south.

Only a few hardy ornamentals were known, so the shrubbery consisted of exotics such as orange trees, jasmine, pomegranates and oleanders, all in pots or tubs. Some of these tubs were so large and heavy they had to be wheeled into the garden on special vehicles. In late spring, hedges would be trimmed, the low ones edging the beds and the high ones composed of trees planted along the *allées* and called *palissades*. One day's work followed the next according to long-established routine. By November the exotics were wheeled back to the orangerie and gardeners turned to pruning or to indoor tasks such as making straw screens and coverings.

The gardeners, like men in every trade and profession of the time, formed a close group, intermarrying and handing on their jobs from father to son for generations. At the Tuileries, Pierre Le Nôtre, André's grandfather, had been in charge of the upkeep of six parterres (that is, flower gardens, generally level, with the flowers, grass and paths forming a definite design). There the head gardener was one of the Mollets, member of a second famous gardening dynasty always closely associated with the Le Nôtre family.

André's father, Jean, inherited Pierre's job, worked under the Claude Mollet of his day, and in turn became headgardener. One of the Mollets worked for the son-in-law of Diane de Poitiers at Anet in the sixteenth century. Another, André, wrote *Le jardin de plaisir* published in 1651; still another, Claude, was the author of *Théâtre des plants et jardinages*, written in 1610.

André was born March 12, 1613.When he was baptized Madame Claude Mollet was his godmother and the Sieur de Maisonville, superintendent of the royal gardens, his godfather. This group of gardeners did not belong to the guilds because they were on the royal payroll. Jean Le Nôtre was thrifty. He owned his house on the Faubourg-Saint-Honoré, whence a short lane led directly to his place of work, the Tuileries gardens. The *faubourg* (a part of the city outside the walls) was then on the outskirts of Paris, bounded by a stream, beyond which were meadows and farms with tilled fields. It is likely that André as a little boy waded across the stream and walked to the farms beyond to watch the hoeing, planting and harvesting of crops. Farming was carried on practically as it had been in Roman days and with tools and methods that were almost as primitive.

During the summer, then as now, amateur and professional gardeners visited each other to exchange plants and ideas; on winter evenings they would gather indoors to talk about their work. Among them would be Simon Bouchard, husband of André's eldest sister Françoise, and Pierre Desgots, who had married the second sister Elizabeth, and members of the Mollet family. With them might have been Jacques Boyceau de la Barauderie, nephew of the first Sieur de la Barauderie, author of *Traité du jardinage*, published in 1638, who had designed the parterres in the royal gardens of the Louvre, Tuileries and Luxembourg, many of which André was to do over entirely. An enthusiastic gardener of the time was Guy de La Brosse, physician to Louis XIII, who had a garden of herbs and wrote a book about them.

Another was Monsieur Morin, who was also a physician with the title of *associé botaniste* and whose collection of anemones and tulips was well known. Of the latter he had ten thousand—a fashionable and expensive hobby in the days soon after the tulip mania of 1634, when as much as three thousand florins had been paid for two bulbs.

With young André growing up among them and showing great promise, the older gardeners naturally discussed what training would be best for him. It was a time when education was highly specialized, when only the most clever knew how to read and write, and when sons followed their father's callings. The Sieur de la Barauderie had set forth in a book the qualifications and education he thought a gardener should have—and evidently Le Nôtre's parents agreed with his ideas for it was almost exactly the training they gave their son. De la Barauderie declared that no one should undertake to be a gardener or design gardens without thorough preparation, that the prospective gardener should learn how to read and write, should know arithmetic and should learn to draw though he need not study sculpture or painting. Drawing was necessary in order to trace designs on the ground, that is, to carry out patterns in flower beds which originated in embroidery. These patterns had been elaborated by the Mollet family. The future gardener was also to learn geometry in order to be able to measure paths and beds. If he showed promise, he was to study architecture to enable him to design terraces, balustrades and garden houses. Besides all this theoretical training he was to learn how to make various kinds of stakes for supporting plants and keeping them in shape, how to plant and clip hedges and *palissades*. In regard to raising flowers and vegetables, he was to learn how to sow seeds, force and transplant, retard and conserve, and how to whiten and soften vegetables such as cardoons, chicory and alisanders (*Smyrnium olusatrum*). Moreover he was to learn about soils and be able to predict the weather, which had been considered a necessary accomplishment of gardeners since Roman days.

When he was still a youth André showed so much talent for drawing it was thought he would become a painter. Though it must have been a disappointment to his parents to have their son leave the family calling, they arranged for him to study with Simon Vouet, then painter-in-chief to

Bust of Le Nôtre by Coysevox in the Church of St. Roch.

Louis XIII, who took lessons from Vouet and made portraits of his courtiers in pastels. Though Vouet was a mediocre painter, he was evidently a good teacher, if we are to judge by the distinction his pupils attained; for besides Le Nôtre he taught Louis Lerambert, the sculptor, and Charles Le Brun. In his biographical sketch of Vouet in *Les hommes illustrés,* Charles Perrault noted, "Monsieur Le Nôtre learned to draw from him and owes him part of his great ability in the fine ordering of parterres and other ornaments of gardening."

Due to his natural gifts and helped by his training, Le Nôtre was deft at rendering plans. He would color them delicately and execute the details clearly and minutely. When the outlines of his great plans, such as the one of Versailles, are studied, they show the unity, clarity and fine sense of proportion that characterized the pictures he created not in paint on canvas but in living plants and out-of-doors.

Vouet's pupils assisted him in preparing cartoons for tapestries and mixing colors, and, after they became skilled, they filled in details on the murals he was painting for churches and for private homes of ministers of state. He worked for Cardinal Richelieu and for the ministers d'Effiat, Bouillon, and Servien, who all lined their pockets while in office and then built themselves magnificent homes with the spoils.

Undoubtedly Le Nôtre's natural taste for art was stimulated during his years in Vouet's studio. Madame Vouet, an Italian, was also a painter and collaborated with her husband. Both had traveled widely. Vouet had gone to Constantinople in the suite of Monsieur de Harly, the French ambassador to the Sublime Porte, and had made a portrait of the Sultan (either Ahmed III or Mohammed I). He brought back drawings of terraced gardens on the Bosphorus, tiled mosques, minarets, and fountains trickling out of shell-shaped basins. In his designs, Le Nôtre used the broken curves and other gleanings from Near Eastern art. Later, when there was so much interest in Turkey that Molière introduced a Turkish ballet into *Le bourgeois gentilhomme* and Racine wrote Bajázet, Le Nôtre bought a Koran, histories of the Ottoman Empire and of the Turks, and a book entitled *La vie des perses.* He also learned about the art of other countries from the many visitors who came to see Vouet, and by studying engravings of Italian works of art in portfolios on the shelves of the studio. Thus, although he did not go abroad himself until he went to England in 1660 and to Italy in 1680, when he was already sixty-seven years old, Le Nôtre knew the art of other countries as well as he knew earlier French art.

By the time Le Nôtre was twenty-two years old, he realized that gardening, not painting, was to be his medium of expression and true vocation. As a further preparation for his chosen career he studied architecture. It is thought he studied either with Le Mercier, who had designed Rueil for Cardinal Richelieu (where Vouet had painted the frescoes), or with François Mansart, since the Mansart and Le Nôtre families were friendly and Le Nôtre later took a fatherly interest in young Jules Hardouin-Mansart. Also, early in his career Le Nôtre laid out the park at Maisons where François Mansart designed a chateau that is greatly admired to this day.

Combining the professions of architect and gardener, Le Nôtre was the supreme architect of gardens. The structures he designed include the stairways and supporting wall of the orangerie at Versailles, the ramp at Chantilly and the terraces at Saint-Germain and the Tuileries; these are all admired for their strength, simplicity, and the way they serve their purpose or, to use a modern term, their functionalism. There is also little doubt that Le Nôtre was the creator of buildings that were credited to his colleagues, for he was consulted on many projects but was so careful not to antagonize anyone that he frequently let others carry out his sketches and ideas.

This happened in the planning of the orangerie at Versailles. Apparently the King had turned to young Mansart for a plan but was not satisfied with it; so he asked Le Nôtre to try his hand. Le Nôtre excused himself saying: "Your Majesty knows my talents are limited to the composition of gardens. I am not an architect." The King knew this was merely a tactful evasion, that Le Nôtre simply did not wish to offend Mansart. He continued to press Le Nôtre, and a few days later Le Nôtre appeared at the King's levée with a rolled-up plan. Louis said, "I see you have a sketch. What is it?" "Sire," answered Le Nôtre, "last night the orangerie appeared to me in a dream and I got up immediately and made a drawing of it." Mansart, one assumes, could hardly be offended by a dream. Lafond de Saint-Yenne (quoted by Lucien Corpechot in *Les jardins de l'intelligence*, 1912) reports that the King called for Mansart and ordered him to carry out Le Nôtre's scheme.

After André had spent two years studying architecture it was thought he had sufficient training to begin his career as a gardener. His father applied to the King for an order to have his own position descend to his son

33

and for additional funds with which to pay him. While waiting for the order and emoluments to come through, André went to work in the Tuileries with his father, his relatives and old family friends. From entries in the *Comptes des bâtiments sous le règne de Louis XIV* published by Colbert to show the public how and where money was spent, it is known exactly what Le Nôtre's duties at the Tuileries were. An entry dated 1667, when he was already famous as a landscape architect and undoubtedly had a staff to assist him, says he was in charge of the newly planted parterres in front of the Tuileries, where he had to see that terraces as well as *allées* and walks were cleaned, beaten and raked. He also had to see that the green shrubs in the parterres were cultivated, fertilized and garnished "in season with flowers of the same kind as are there, which he will have lifted, replaced, covered and regarnished at his expense." Another item is "the upkeep of the Spanish jasmine hedge for the whole length of the wall of the terrace, of the mulberry *allée*, and furnishing of fertilizer and other necessities." For this work he was paid a total of eight thousand *livres*. (At the beginning of the twentieth century, a seventeenth century *livre* was figured to be the equivalent of an American dollar.)

Le Nôtre was in charge of the upkeep of these gardens all his life and saw to it that his nephews, Claude Desgots and Michel Le Bouteux, who were his assistants, would inherit this task after his death.

In addition to their own work, André and his father carried on Simon Bouchard's work after his death. They did this to keep this post in the family and enable the widow, Françoise, and her children to maintain their home near the orangerie and the income of twelve hundred *livres*. This was typical of how members of the family helped each other and how Le Nôtre himself behaved all his life. Father and son must have been superlatively able, for the English diarist John Evelyn, himself a keen gardener, wrote of the parterre at the Tuileries that "being kept with all imaginable accurateness, as to orangerie, precious shrubs and rare fruits, it seemed a Paradise."

When the King's order came through in January 1637, it mentioned that "the King Louis XIII had heard good and praiseworthy reports about the person of his dear André Le Nôtre, of his sense, competence, loyalty, integrity and experience in regard to gardening." The order provided that the requested increase in salary be given to Jean, who was to give André his share; and with this appointment went a lodging in the park, provided for all artists and artisans employed in the palace, stables or in the upkeep of the gardens. Thus André, now a handsome young fellow, moved from the family home into an apartment of his own, close to his fellow workers and colleagues. Here lived his friend, the young sculptor Lerambert, and here too for two years lived the painter Nicolas Poussin before he returned to Italy.

Soon Le Nôtre was called to work for private clients, including the planning of a garden in Paris for Monsieur Tom Bonneau, "*president à la chambre des comptes*," who owned a fine collection of botanical and horticultural books. When the young garden architect came to the house he would often find Jean de La Quintinie, a young lawyer, whom Tom Bonneau had engaged as tutor for his son, in the library deep in a book. Eventually, de La Quintinie gave up law to become an authority on grafting and growing fruit trees; later he designed the vegetable gardens at Vaux-le-Vicomte, Chantilly and Versailles. Today the vegetable garden at Versailles is part of the *École d'horticulture* and in it there is a statue of de La Quintinie with a scion in one hand and a grafting knife in the other. He and Le Nôtre undoubtedly discussed horticultural subjects but they must also have discussed their beliefs, for, like Le Nôtre, de La Quintinie showed how deeply he was influenced by Descartes when he wrote in his *Instructions pour les jardins fruitiers et potagers*, translated by John Evelyn as *The Compleat Gard'ner:* "I have endeavored to reason with the greatest evidence I could, the better to confirm the instructions I give and which I found only upon very frequent and very long observations by myself in all parts of gardening without taking anything upon trust, upon the report of any other person."

Le Nôtre deeply loved his work and continued to study all his life. He undoubtedly gained ideas for composition from the study of paintings as have many landscape architects. In his youth he commissioned Poussin, then considered "the most famous painter in Christendom" (but not popular at court), to paint a picture for him; later he bought more of his work as well as Claude Lorraine's, whose landscapes are almost romantic in spirit. Le Nôtre admired the way these two artists rendered sky and space, their handling of light so that it transfused the scenery, the clarity of intention and the absence of crowding. He adapted these rhythms and spacings to his own field of work. Besides buying paintings, Le Nôtre collected engravings of earlier French houses and gardens by du Cerceau and, in addition, Italian and French paintings and sculptures.

A man's library reveals his taste and Le Nôtre's showed he was open-minded and curious. (The items in his library are listed in the *Bulletin de la société de l'histoire du l'art françois*, 1911, pp. 228-238, 260-271, 274-282.) Besides the Bible, biographies of saints and ecclesiastical histories, he had books on the English religious reformers, one on Calvin and another on Luther. He gleaned ideas for his work from all forms of art: he was the first in France to collect Chinese porcelains; he had a book on the French Embassies to Japan and to China by Father Quelquer. There were also such less scholarly books as *Histoires galantes*. Kept handy on his walnut table was a book on the principles of architecture and two dictionaries. Martin Lister, an English zoologist who visited Le Nôtre's art collection, remarked there was no book on natural history. This was not strange, for Le Nôtre's work was not based on nature but, true to his Cartesian principles, was entirely intellectual.

One day when André was in the Tuileries, supervising the drawing of patterns on the ground to outline a *parterre de broderie*, a feminine shadow fell across the bed. Looking up, he saw the smiling face of blond, blue-eyed Françoise Langlois with whom he had played in the Tuileries gardens when both were children. Her father was François Langlois, Sieur de Hamel, councilor to the French artillery and governor of the pages in the royal stables. In time they were affianced. According to the custom of the day the marriage contract was drawn, signed and witnessed in the bride's home. It shows that the young couple received many valuable gifts and were well provided for financially.

On a cold, pleasant day in January 1640, the wedding party, composed of friends, relatives and associates, repaired to the newly built Church of Saint-Roch, not far from their homes, for the religious ceremony. The wedding feast probably took place in the restaurant belonging to Renaud, situated in the old moat beyond the Tuileries. There was good food and wine, for these *bourgeois* lived well. After the feast the bride and groom were escorted to their home in the Tuileries, which had been furnished with rich gifts and a lavish trousseau.

There Le Nôtre and his wife led a happy home life. Though André was dashing in appearance and vivacious and lived at a court where moral taboos were practically non-existent, there was never a breath of scandal about him. Evidently the directing of energy into strictly disciplined channels was as true of his private life as was the measure and control of his gardens. Françoise had a sweet disposition, got on well with her own and her husband's family, and was an excellent and frugal housekeeper. Over a period of nineteen years, André and Françoise had three children who must have died in infancy for there is no mention of them in any of the deeds signed by Le Nôtre in regard to his properties. Not having children of their own, they fathered their nephews and nieces, and a godchild. Le Nôtre was probably often away from home in the course of his work. However, his wife was not alone, for after the death of Jean Le Nôtre, André's mother came to live with the couple and stayed until she died.

André Le Nôtre and his wife were wealthy. Besides the large sums of money André earned all his life from private clients, he received lavish gifts as well as his pay from the King. It has been estimated that his annual income was about 35,000 *livres*. In addition, both he and his wife had inherited land and presents from their parents: his property was in the rue du Faubourg-Saint-Honoré and hers covered almost one whole side of the present avenue des Champs-Elysées.

They lived very comfortably in their richly and artistically furnished home in the Tuileries gardens. Françoise's attempts at restraining her husband from spending too much money on his art collection must have been a family joke, for in his will he wrote of "the said lady his wife, who has kept a close hand in the conservation of the possessions they have saved by her good conduct, for the said testator was always inclined to incur expenses for his collection of curios without thinking of saving but only of glory and honor."

CHAPTER IV

GARDENS BEFORE ANDRÉ LE NÔTRE'S TIME

S OME SCHOLARS HAVE claimed that the French classical garden already existed when Le Nôtre came upon the scene and that he did not produce anything new. If this is so, then it makes just as much sense to say that the French language had reached perfection at the time of François Villon, Pierre de Ronsard or Michel de Montaigne.

The old gardens belonging to the French kings were in a quite literal sense Le Nôtre's own heritage for it was his ancestors who had worked the soil and shaped it—as he himself had done in his youth—planted the shrubs and trimmed the trees in the walled enclosures. He knew from hearsay, from pictures and from the very stones themselves how the nobles and kings had changed their châteaux from fortified castles to pleasant residences and he lived to see these residences become resplendent symbols of power. He was so saturated with the knowledge of how these gardens had developed from within the area of the feudal castle and how they had acquired their Italian features, and he knew the history of each of them so intimately that his work inevitably had its roots in the past. However, he was so much a man of his day and so original an artist that he could transform an inherited scheme and make gardens which expressed the attitudes of his time.

In his layout Le Nôtre retained the scheme that had been developed by his predecessors, from the fortified castle with its moat and its series of courts, called baileys, separated by walls or by moats with drawbridges. Within the prescribed formula there could be infinite variations in the handling of the scheme. Le Nôtre's intentions were so definite and were carried out with such clarity that the sources of inspiration are evident. The entrance driveway inside the property led to an entrance court (corresponding to the outermost bailey of the fortified castle) which in turn led to a second court directly in front of the château and then into a third courtyard similar to the inner bailey; this last was often surrounded on three sides by the château and its wings or by the dwelling and its stables. Poultry-yards and stables for cattle (called *basses-courts*) were, as was customary, at some distance. The gardens were on the opposite side from the approaches. Facing the garden there was always a terrace where the battlements had been and on a slightly lower level there was often an ornamental watercourse to repeat the theme of the moat which had surrounded the castle in olden days. The scheme whereby the house stands between the entrance and the garden is maintained to this day in France, where houses are set close to the street and the gardens take up the whole area in back of the house.

During the Middle Ages, gardens were sometimes situated within the precincts of the fortifications, which often covered large areas—as at the Tuileries and Amboise—and were like crowded villages. When times became slightly less perilous, the gardens were often placed outside the fortifications and were reached from the house by a covered walk. To protect them from incursions of wild animals and robbers, they would be enclosed with high walls, frequently crenelated—just as the medieval battlements had been. Such walls confined the view to the garden.

To judge from illustrations in illuminated manuscripts, scenes on tapestries, and from descriptions by contemporary writers, these gardens, created by men handicapped by lack of experience and suitable materials, had the childlike charm that characterizes certain primitive paintings. The idea of the garden was to provide an area away from the dark castle, where one might stroll, read poetry, and make love in sweet-smelling air sparkling with sunlight and musical with the sound of birds.

These first gardens were like roofless outdoor rooms. As in many contemporary paintings, there was no representation of perspective.

Artists had not learned to eliminate the unessential, or the petty and disturbing elements in order to produce a harmonious, unified result. So many objects were crowded into a small space that sometimes corners had to be cut away from flower beds to allow a path to encircle a fountain. Moreover, trees were trained into espaliers flat against walls or pruned into globes or pyramids so as not to take up too much space or cut off sunlight. At that time and for many years to come, no one ornament or plant was either accented or subordinated, so that many features competed for attention.

Few medieval gardens remained for young Le Nôtre actually to see. Forms more suitable to great cathedrals and huge fortified castles were used with quaint effect in these little gardens because the designers knew no others. Thus a stream of water would gush from gargoyle-like spouts and a summer-house covered with honeysuckle or clematis would have a pointed roof supported by Gothic arches.

The flower beds were edged with clipped plants of rosemary, lavender, hyssop or box, a horticultural custom descended from Roman days; within the beds were herbs for healing and flavor, including marjoram, savory, dill and fennel, needed by the mistress in the castle. There were also a few strongly scented flowers—hyacinths, roses, carnations and lilies. Exotic plants, seeds and cuttings brought home by Crusaders were often present. In the center might be a pond where fish could be raised and kept fresh for the table.

When the garden was large it might consist of several department-like rooms, separated from each other by brightly painted fences of woven wattle (wicker) or of latticework. In larger gardens, coming a little later in history, a favorite layout was one composed of squares, as in a checkerboard, each having a distinctive design (later called *parterre à fleurs*). Le Nôtre could still see these at Blois. Sometimes the designs would be based on heraldic symbols or geometric figures; or there might be a miniature maze, a popular idea derived from stories of Crete and its Minotaur.

By the fifteenth century, travelers returning from Italy brought back stories of a way of life far more emancipated from fear than that which was lived within fortified walls in France; they told of lovely gardens designed by the great painters Michelangelo and Raphael and the architects Michelozzi,

Working drawing of grillwork on gate at Versailles.

Buontalenti and Vignola for the wealthy merchant princes of Florence, Siena and Rome.

The origin of the Italian garden was entirely different from the French for it grew out of the villa or farm generally situated on an elevation overlooking land laid out in a series of terraces. Since the villa was therefore high above the surrounding country, views from its terraces were not confined to the garden but embraced the hills and valleys of the neighborhood. In comparison with the vastness of later French parks, Italian gardens were small. Because the land was uneven, both house and garden, though balanced, were not always, like the French, symmetrical. Another difference was that the Italians had green gardens, planted with box, yew, laurel and evergreen oaks, whereas the French, though they used these plants, also had many deciduous trees and shrubs and from earliest times enlivened their beds with the color of flowers.

Italian artists imported by French kings to embellish their estates brought with them the idea that house and garden should form a unit

fig. 4.^e

Sketch for the palissade of the Theatre de l'Eau at Versailles (left),
and for a palissade at the Trianon (right).

in design. Also they taught the French antecedents of Le Nôtre (as they have taught a goodly part of the world from India to California) to build terraces and embankments. They showed them how to pleach hornbeam and beech trees (that is, to interweave the branches of one tree with those of another on the opposite side of a path) in order to form a tunnel of living green; and they taught them the art of topiary, that is, how to train and clip woody plants into fantastic shapes either geometric or animal. This shaping of shrubs had been popular under the Roman empire and had been practiced by the French though not with the same intricacy or skill. The Italians brought with them new ideas in design for beds, garden-houses and water effects, for they had undergone their Renaissance while the French were still working with earlier Gothic models.

The first colony of Italian artists was brought to France late in the fifteenth century by Charles VII and housed at Amboise in Touraine on the river Loire. Among them was a Neapolitan, Pasciello de Mercoliano, reputed to be skilled in laying out gardens. After Charles died in 1498, his

Jardin de la Maison de Mr. de St. Poange rüe des petits Champs,
De l'invention de Mons.r le Nautre

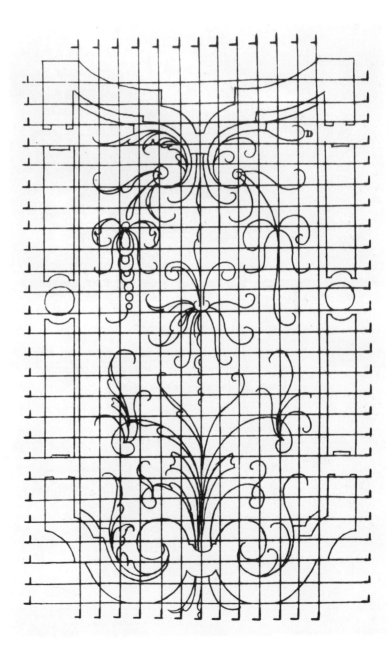

Left: Sketch of parterre de broderie for the garden of de St. Poange Right: Working drawing of a parterre from *La theorie et le pratique du jardinage* by Le Blond.

successor, Louis XII, continued to employ the Italian and commissioned him to make over the gardens at Amboise and Blois. At Amboise, Mercoliano built colonnaded cloisters to enclose the garden, which was situated inside the large fortified enclosure high above the river. At Blois, where the castle is also on a hill, the garden was outside the fortified area and was reached by a roofed gallery leading from the house and crossing the moat. After the construction at Blois was finished, Italian gardeners were imported to cultivate the gardens. Contemporary with these buildings was the great château at Gaillon, overlooking the Seine and owned by Louis XII's prime minister, Cardinal Archbishop of Rouen. All these gardens were well known to Le Nôtre.

Later, other colonies of Italians were brought to Fontainebleau by Francis I and Henry II. Under their influence a type of architecture developed which had a Gothic foundation and Italianate ornamentation. Gradually the French fused the two and created a distinctive and delightful style, some of it in Francis I's time and some in the period of Henry II.

By the middle of the sixteenth century, French artists, now far more skilled than they were before the introduction of the Italians, were to have the opportunity to create a truly French garden. For when Diane de Poitiers, Duchesse de Valentinois and mistress of Henry II of France, decided to rebuild her château of Anet (at Dreux about forty-eight miles west of Paris), she called upon French artists to carry out her ideas. She was considered the arbiter of taste and manners and it was in her entourage that young Mary Stuart, later Queen of Scotland, was brought up. Perhaps Diane called upon French artists instead of Italian in order to antagonize her rival, the Queen, Catherine de Médicis, who was Italian. Whatever her motives, she was the first to employ French artists and from the year 1549 to 1553 Anet became, under her patronage, the center of French art, as Vaux-le-Vicomte and Versailles became later on.

There was a new lightness and gaiety of motifs at Anet. It was new to dedicate a château to a woman. Diane had a beautiful figure, was a good swimmer and fine horsewoman and followed the hounds with the King. Because of her name and fondness for hunting, the courtyard of the castle was dominated by a statue of the goddess Diana made by one of the greatest

Sketch of a parterre from Le Blond.

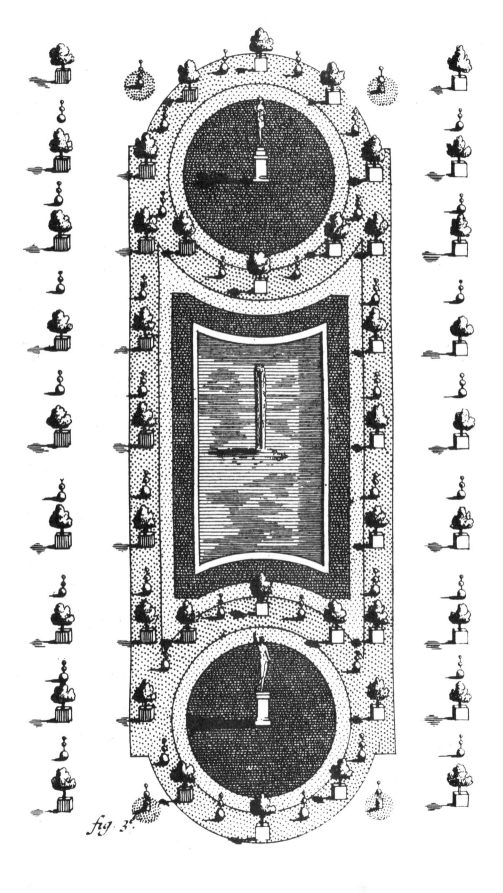

fig. 3.

French sculptors, Jean Goujon, and rumor said the lady herself had posed for it. Over the tympanum of the gateway was a relief of the goddess by Benvenuto Cellini, and above that a clock; still higher, hunting dogs bayed on either side of a stag which struck the hours with its hooves. This gateway is now in the *École des beaux-arts* in Paris.

At Anet, for the first time in France, garden and castle formed a unit; in fact, the château was strongly influenced by the garden. Also for the first time the entrance courts were on the near side of the building and the garden on the far side. A third new feature, to become a rule in the grammar of garden design, was placing the central garden path on an axis with the center of the building.

The garden was sunk and the pattern of the beds consisted of symmetrical, rectangular shapes. Neither of these features was new. As at Blois and other gardens of the time, there was an arcaded loggia on three sides of the garden. On the side opposite the house and beyond the loggia, was a minstrel gallery with a swimming bath for Diane on its lower story. Beyond were a heronry, an orangerie, and aviaries, the last two being innovations from Italy. There was also a tennis court for athletic Diane and the King.

Anet descended to Diane's son-in-law, the Duc d'Aumale, who employed the Mollets as his gardeners.

Inspired by these achievements, other nobles had their castles and grounds modernized or created new ones. In each instance there was an effort to have some original and outstanding feature, all of which gave an impetus to architecture and garden design. At Vallèry, belonging to Henry II, there was a garden similar to the one belonging to his mistress at Anet. The novelty here was a watercourse down the center, the timid début of a feature later to be expanded by Le Nôtre.

An important source for houses and gardens of the sixteenth century is the collection of engravings by Jacques Androuet du Cerceau, published in English in 1909 under the title *French Chateaux and Gardens in the XVIth Century*, edited by W. H. Ward. According to this book, the château of Verneuil was originally built by M. de Boulainvillers in 1565 and later passed into other hands and was frequently altered. Du Cerceau made detailed drawings of the house and its gardens, which were architecturally important. There were several buildings on different levels. Innovations in

The Tuileries in Le Nôtre's youth.

later versions of the gardens, which were more elaborate than the ones at Vallèry, were terraces supported by embankments, some margined with balustrades. Stairways led from one terrace to the next and at the lowest level, situated at right angles to the principal building, was a watercourse. At one end of this canal-like waterway was a decorative tunnel and on the far bank a garden house reached by a bridge. A step forward at Verneuil was that all the beds formed a unified design. As a kind of reflection of the drive toward unity in politics, unity in the arts was being introduced. Henry IV, he of the white plume, who had said Paris was worth a mass, made an effective move toward bringing all factions in France into harmony when he became a Catholic in order to be king and in so doing reduced the friction between Catholics and Protestants, the cause of so many civil wars.

Not far from Saint-Cloud was Rueil, a palace with extra-

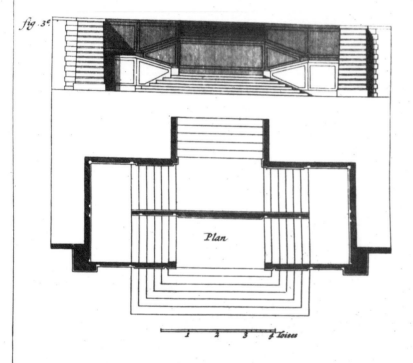

Grand Escalier du Jardin des Tuilleries
Elevation

fig. 3.

Plan

1   2   3   4 *Toises*

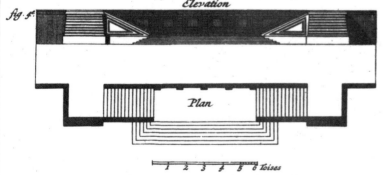

Petit Escalier du Jardin des Tuilleries
Elevation

fig. 4.

Plan

1   2   3   4   5   6 *Toises*

Sketch for the Grand Stairways
at the Tuileries (left), and St.
Cloud and Luxembourg (right).

Grand Escalier du Jardin de S.ᵗ Cloud
Elevation

fig. 1.ᵉʳ

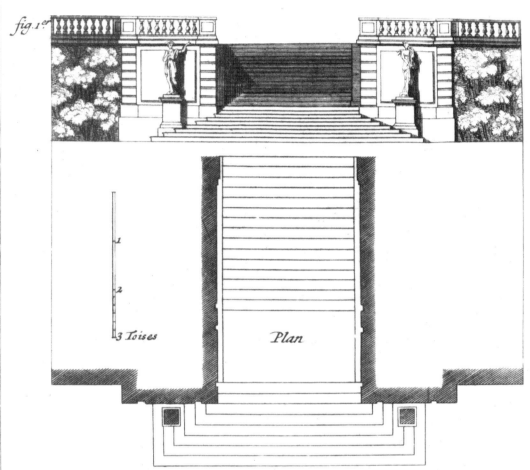

Plan

1

2

3 Toises

Escalier du Jardin de Luxembourg
Elevation

fig. 2.ᵉ

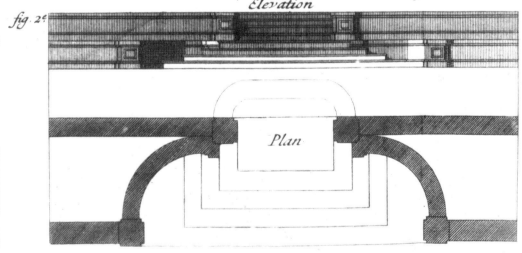

Plan

1   2   3   4   5 Toises

ordinarily long wings, belonging to Cardinal Richelieu, who spent huge sums of money developing it. Jean Le Nôtre worked at Rueil and André knew the place well. For the first time, the surroundings beyond the garden proper entered into the decorative scheme; and the houses of the nearby village were built in the same style of architecture as the castle, namely with steep roofs, stuccoed walls and stone coigns. Modern features were cross axes made of paths and forming part of the design that broke the stiffness and at the same time provided means for viewing the garden from different approaches. The enthusiastic descriptions of John Evelyn and other visitors show that the French had gone far beyond their Italian teachers in developing the park. There was a pavilion in the garden, where Richelieu held council while *hallebardiers* of his household guard tramped back and forth between box-edged flower beds and down tree-lined *allées*. It is known that the *allées* were very long, for when Queen Anne came to Rueil after Richelieu's death, she drove down them in a carriage accompanied by a poet who read aloud to her. In the evening she walked in the garden where an Italian singer entertained her.

Among Italian garden ornaments elaborated by the French was the *parterre de broderie*. The designs were taken from books of embroidery such as *Le livre dict patron de lingerie*, published at Lyon in 1549, whence had also come the name. They were a delight to Claude Mollet who was undoubtedly highly skilled at executing them. He and his sons made original designs and assembled them in a book called *Théàtre des plants et jardinages* with text by Claude, finished in 1610 but not published until 1652, under the aegis of Fouquet. The figures in these patterns were distinguished by a nomenclature of their own, such as *feuillages*, *moresques* and *arabesques*. Originally Mollet had executed them with herbaceous plants but as his enthusiasm waxed and the designs became increasingly complicated, this was no longer possible. He continued to make his outlines with box; but instead of plants for the fillings, he used colored earths for the red and the yellow, and iron filings for black.

These patterns have continued to be popular in French gardens but in a much simplified form. The gardener first divides the area with strings tied to little sticks pushed in the ground, and then draws the pattern with a stick on earth that has previously been smoothed with a rake. Beside him are baskets filled with seedling plants ready to be set in the ground to carry out the design. Le Nôtre used the embroidery patterns because they were fashionable and popular but he did not admire them and said they were fit only to amuse wet nurses who were confined to the house and had to look down on the garden from a second-story window.

Gradually French gardens grew out of their cramped areas within high walls and spread out on the landscape. The ornaments, such as water, terraces, garden houses and patterns of parterres, were carried out with increasing skill and designed with greater inventiveness. It remained for André Le Nôtre with his feeling for unity and balance, his infallible sense of proportion and insistence on broad, sunlit spaces, wide expanses of sky and unimpeded vistas, to bring the French classical garden to perfection.

CHAPTER V

OUTSTANDING EARLY WORK

URING the last years of Louis XIII's reign and the early part of Louis XIV's, wealthy nobles of the robe and of the sword, as well as the royal family, were building fine private houses in Paris and in the country, so there was much work for architects, contractors and decorators. At that period no merchants or bankers seem to have built conspicuous places in the country.

Commissions come to a landscape gardener for various reasons, not for talent alone. Besides being able to imagine and execute his work, the artist has to be on friendly terms with his colleagues; to satisfy his employer, he must be able to make concessions and renounce some of his pet ideas. Le Nôtre was obviously a master at pleasing clients. Besides his ability he had charm, self-control and wit. Moreover, as we know from his own words, he was very sure of himself, and, in turn, inspired confidence.

Later in his career, after he had worked at Versailles, Chantilly and Saint-Cloud, he could insist either on having his own way or not doing the work at all. When working for the Grande Mademoiselle, he thought she should cut down some of her trees to open a view, whereas she preferred to leave the trees so she could stroll under them in the moonlight, so temporarily they parted company. Again at Versailles, he evaded doing work he did not admire, such as the grotto designed by Perrault or the absurd bosquet thought up by Madame de Montespan.

The Bishop's Garden at Meaux, showing the design in the shape of a miter.

From his childhood Le Nôtre was closely associated with architects and contractors, especially those engaged in work for the state and the great ministers. Many of his colleagues had observed him at his studies or in his work at the Tuileries and knew his ability. Some of the most distinguished ones were his contemporaries: Louis Mansart, the architect of Maisons, where Le Nôtre did the gardens, was fifteen years his senior; Louis Le Vau, who designed much of the royal architecture until his death in 1670, was only one year older; and Charles Le Brun, virtual dictator of the arts under Colbert, was six years his junior. Le Vau had designed Monsieur Tom Bonneau's house, where Le Nôtre laid out the garden. Perhaps this was his first collaboration with Le Vau, with whom he was to work on several projects and at Versailles for nine years.

The design of the gardens of Claude de Bouillon at Wideville may have been given to Le Nôtre through the influence of Vouet, who made the cartoons for the decorations of de Bouillon's city house and country house and also for his grotto. These gardens still exist and are much admired by the French, who speak of the place as *un jardin délicieux*. The principal garden is centered on the house and composed of one unit in four parts. The beds are of turf, a type of parterre called *á l'Anglaise*, and in each is a large graceful *fleur-de-lis* carried out in box, while along the margins at pivotal points are evergreens clipped in fantastic shapes. Standing at the far end of the main axis, in a semicircular niche and against a background of woods, is a pavilion called *la nymphée*, a combination grotto and garden house, a building much admired at the time. Despite the smallness of the garden, the hand of Le Nôtre is seen in the sense of space, and in the simplicity and charm of the details, such as the baroque curves that round the corners of the near beds, and in the way that two beds, one round, the other somewhat diamond-shaped, break the severity of the central axis without destroying its strength.

This plan could be adapted for a small garden on a level piece of land almost anywhere. So could the plan of the episcopal garden at Meaux, also still in existence; this one Le Nôtre laid out at about the same time as Wideville, in the years 1643-44, when he was thirty years old, during the incumbency of Monseigneur Séguier. The idea for the garden at Meaux is witty and original, for Le Nôtre made the outlines in the shape of a bishop's miter and the intersection of the paths formed a bishop's cross. Though the area is small, the most was made of every part; there is even a scant wood in front of the city fortifications which bound the garden on one side. Later, when Bossuet, beloved preacher of the age, had this as his living, he was called "the eagle of Meaux." A stairway led to the terrace built on top of the ramparts, and there stood a little building, called *Le Cabinet de Bossuet*, in which he could meditate and write undisturbed.

When Le Nôtre was called in, the episcopal residence was an old unsymmetrical building with a portico on one side. Le Nôtre centered the garden on one of the arches of this portico. As at Wideville, the parterre was divided by two intersecting paths into four beds of turf, but these beds

The Luxembourg Gardens, an engraving by Rigaud, 1729.

are not equal in size because the farther ones are rounded out to form the upper part of the miter. The central axis is broken with a pool placed at the intersection of the two paths, perhaps to represent a jewel in the miter. The beds are outlined with a border of flowers; throughout the garden there are accents made by clipped evergreens. As in all Le Nôtre's work, the garden is framed, first by an inner line of trees clipped geometrically, then outside this by a second line of trees allowed to spread naturally. Between the little wood and the old city walls is a shaded walk.

This episcopal garden was so delightful that Le Nôtre was commissioned to design two others, one at Bourges and another at Castres.

One of the charms of Paris today are its numerous parks. Most of them originated as private gardens and many of the old ones were glorified by Le Nôtre. At the outset of his career, before he was thirty, Le Nôtre was called to work at the Luxembourg by Gaston, Duc d'Orléans, who had heard him highly commended, perhaps by François Mansart, the architect of the new wing at his château of Blois, which was built in 1635–40. The Duke, an unscrupulous but fascinating man, had plotted with his mother, Marie de Medicis, against his only brother, her son Louis XIII. As a result, both were sent into exile, the Queen out of France, but Gaston no farther than Blois.

However, his daughter, the Grande Mademoiselle, was in constant attendance at court and when in Paris lived at the Luxembourg. The palace had been built from 1615–20, for Marie de Medicis, on the foundation of an older building. It was in the Italian style, designed by Salomon de Brosse, who also laid out the gardens (though Boyceau designed the parterres). They were wider than long, due to the lie of the land. Le Nôtre made changes in the lateral portions. John Evelyn describes the park in 1644 when these changes had been completed, mentioning a grove of tall elms transversed by star-shaped *allées*, each with a large fountain in it. A plan by Gomboust made in 1652 confirms Evelyn's description.

Today much of the park has been absorbed by the city, but part of the lateral portion is a charming, intimate park open to the public. The Luxembourg palace now houses the French Senate; nonetheless, children sail their boats in the large central fountain of the old portion of the garden and play tennis and other ball games or watch Punch-and-Judy shows in some of the room-like enclosures. Each of the areas is enclosed by trees, the remains of Le Nôtre's groves. To keep the ground dry it is covered with gravel. The trees deaden the sounds of the city; so old men doze over their papers and babies sleep in their carriages undisturbed by the honking of auto-mobiles or the rumble of city traffic.

Voltaire is the authority for attributing the park at the old castle of Vincennes to Le Nôtre, who must have worked there while Mazarin was in residence. The minister had asked Le Vau to remodel the castle and make it more comfortable, and Le Nôtre to surround it with elaborate terraces enclosed by woods, for he hoped the King would use Vincennes as a country residence. However, instead of coming here to a gloomy place but with the advantage of being eight miles from Paris, Louis went twelve miles to Versailles, where he built a shining new palace for himself.

About ten miles from Paris and a slight distance from the sinuous banks of the Seine, a milk-white castle rises, now called Maisons-Laffitte, in a pleasant suburb known for horse-racing. In Le Nôtre's day the palace and

Luxembourg Gardens. The château in the background now houses the French Senate.

gardens were called Maisons; they had been built by René de Longueil, president of the Parliament of Paris and also Superintendent of Finance and *Capitaine de Versailles* and *de Saint-Germain*. The gardéns, as happened so frequently, have been attributed to others but John Evelyn says Le Nôtre was their author. The remnants, moreover, bear his unmistakable signature. The work here was carried out in the years from 1642 to 1650. The house, designed by François Mansart, is considered one of the masterpieces of seventeenth century French architecture.

By this time the fortified castle had changed into a residence suited for luxurious living in the country. Moats had shrunk until they were entirely decorative. Though roofs were still slanted, the round towers had

Château de Wideville. View of parterre.

disappeared, and windows that once were narrow openings, had become wide
and broad. Inside, the château was the first to have a double series of rooms,
lit from one side only and separated by halls; previously there had been only
one series of rooms the whole depth of the house, one leading to the next.

At Maisons, Le Nôtre laid out the first of the parks in his more
mature style and began to include the countryside and its woodlands in the
picture he was creating. Here he demolished a whole village to make way for
the park. The house was set high on a terrace. On the garden side was a
parterre with fountains and beds executed with elaborate *broderie*, while on

the opposite side, stairways and a series of buildings led from the house to the river. Beyond the garden, to dip into Evelyn's diary again, were "extraordinary long walks set with elms and with a noble prospect toward the forest and the Seine, toward Paris." Today, most of the park has been removed to make way for a real-estate development. However, the outlines can still be discerned. The remains of the original wide central *allée* now are flanked with suburban villas; but it still leads to a *rond point*, that is, a circle cut out of the woods. The transverse axis still crosses the principal one at the foot of the main vista.

When the house and garden at Maisons were finished, the King and his mother were entertained there by its owner. This was the first of many visits, so he had the opportunity of seeing Le Nôtre's work while it was developing toward its ultimate perfection.

The château at Raincy, called Livry at the time, built for Jacques Bordier, *intendant des finances*, was finished the same year as Maisons. Reginald Blomfield is almost certain Le Nôtre designed the gardens. If he was their author it would have been the first time the three artists who were later to collaborate at Vaux-le-Vicomte and Versailles worked together on a project, for Le Vau was the architect and Le Brun painted the murals.

This chapter has shown that Le Nôtre's work was known and admired by artists, nobles and royalty as early as the 1640's. There is no basis whatever for the constantly repeated statement that he had done no outstanding work until he was called to Vaux when he was forty-three years old, or that his work there burst upon an astonished world. This misconception undoubtedly arose as part of the flattery bestowed on Fouquet, for crediting him with introducing three great artists to the King made him seem important; but it is not true.

CHAPTER VI

VAUX-LE-VICOMTE BURSTS UPON THE WORLD

ANDRÉ LE NÔTRE came to work at Vaux when he was forty-three years old and on the threshold of a great career. Here he worked with old friends, Le Vau, Le Brun, and other outstanding artists, and also with congenial assistants such as Michel Villedo, the builder. His employer was the brilliant minister and parliamentarian Fouquet, who had excellent taste and was free with money. In such circumstances Le Nôtre was inspired to create a great park, the first that discloses the style of his maturity.

Vaux-le-Vicomte, thirty-two miles from Paris, was created in the short space of five years. Fouquet hurried the work, knowing the King's displeasure at his extravagance. Here the château and its gardens express the classical style of the era of Louis XIV at the moment of its flowering. Smaller than Versailles, it has a more remarkable unity; it is unmarred by excessive display, redundant ornament, or inharmonious additions. Critics consider it more typical of French taste than Versailles. In fact, Vaux was the inspiration for Versailles. On the afternoon of August 17, 1661, Fouquet gave a splendid entertainment there, to display his achievement to the King and the court. To appreciate the drama of this day, we must recall that Fouquet had been

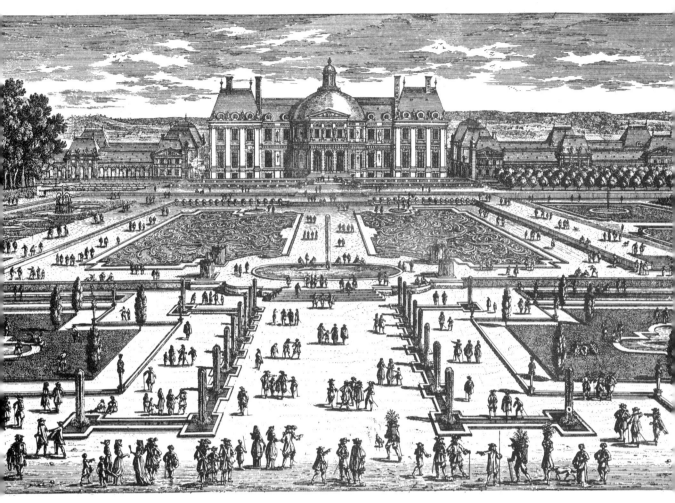

Château at Vaux-le-Vicomte. An engraving by Perelle.

Superintendent of Finance under Mazarin, whom he intended to succeed as *premier ministre*, the virtual ruler of France. He became as wealthy and as powerful as his master, but it was his complete misunderstanding of the young King's character, and not his stealing funds—a custom of the time—that led to his downfall. He thought the King a dullard whose head was filled only with hunting, play-acting, and climbing the palace roof-tops to reach ladies' bedroom windows. He did not realize Louis was biding his time, that he intended to be king in fact, and not to rule through a prime minister.

On that August afternoon he was affronted by Fouquet's pride, by his motto, *Quo non ascendat*, boldly displayed, and by the pictures and symbols representing him as a demigod. Fouquet further irritated the King by living in a style suitable only to royalty or the head of a state; for Fouquet surrounded himself with gifted artists and writers whose patron he was and who flocked to his home, splendid with antiques, jewels, paintings, books and gardens.

After seeing the house, Louis walked onto the terrace; he was accompanied by his host and Le Nôtre was at his side to explain his newest creation. The King was very fond of gardens. As he took in the scene, he was entranced. He saw before him a park in a completely new style.

The sunlit expanse under the broad view of blue sky gave him a sense of space where all was placed in rhythmic balance. The sound of hundreds of fountains could be heard! They dripped from shells and masks, soared into the air with a great rush and curved in arcs of crystal shot through with rainbows. Brightly colored flowers margined some of the beds, filled and hung over the sides of many handsome vases, raised on pedestals, and standing along the marble rims of pools. Statues of gilded lead in the center of fountains glittered from the water splashing over them. Marble *termes* (portion of figures standing on pedestals) gleamed in their whiteness on terraces or against the green of hornbeam hedges clipped almost as smooth as walls of masonry. The topiary of box and yew stood out conspicuously in its dark green tones and bizarre shapes. Orange and bay trees perfumed the air.

As in all gardens supervised by Le Nôtre, the paths and beds were in admirable order, the plants in good health. The *parterre de broderie* in front of the castle was so exact it was like a rug. However the effect was incomplete that day, for the newly planted trees and shrubs were young and far from their intended height.

From the terrace where the King stood the plan was so clear, showing parts so well balanced, that it was like a mathematical problem of Descartes solved in the terms of landscape. Appropriately, the statue of Geometry by Michel Anguier stood in the center of the grand parterre. True to the classical scheme, the central axis led straight out across an ornamental moat and down steps dividing the garden in two, crossed three levels that sloped gently from the house to the river and continued to a wall built in the semi-rustic fashion of a grotto whence issued rushing waters. Beyond the

Vaux-le-Vicomte. The château.

grotto the central axis mounted a grassy hill in a gentle rise to where the gilded statue of Hercules glittered in the sun, accentuated by the dark background formed by an opening into the woods beyond. This statue was two miles from the terrace where the King stood.

After taking in the scene, the King, walking on high, red-heeled shoes, and carrying his long, gold-topped walking stick, proceeded down the central part of the garden. Close to him were Fouquet and Le Nôtre, the King's brother "Monsieur," and the Prince de Condé; behind them on the broad paths came the other guests clad like butterflies in brightly colored clothes, for Louis did not permit anyone to wear black or dark colors at court.

Vaux-le-Vicomte. Grotto and canal. An engraving by Perelle.

It was a momentous walk for Le Nôtre, for France, and the garden art of the world, a walk during which the King planned to build a palace and park to surpass even this one, which he realized was the handsomest in France if not in all Europe. Condé visualized changes he could carry out on his estate at Chantilly and engaged Le Nôtre on the spot. Monsieur thought if a mere minister could have a park like this, he, the King's only brother, was entitled to one; he had it later, at Saint-Cloud, with Le Nôtre as his garden architect. It was many years before Colbert built a sumptuous estate of his own, but eventually at Sceaux he, too, had a magnificent château with Perrault as his architect and Le Nôtre to design the park.

The park at Vaux appeared much smaller than it was. The effect was not of vastness but of an inviting series of features. Openings and exits from one garden to the next were handled so adroitly that the visitor was almost impelled to explore further and was directed where to go without being aware of it.

As they walked along, Le Nôtre explained to the King that all the terraces sloped for the sake of drainage though they appeared to be level, and that the central terrace was higher and consequently more accentuated than the ones on either side. After they had gone some distance, they looked back and noticed that although the foreground was always receding, the château appeared to be at the same distance from the observer. This extraordinary effect was produced by transverse axes made of water, which caused refraction of light and consequent foreshortening of perspectives. It was not in vain that Le Nôtre lived in an age of mathematical explorers such as Descartes and Pascal.

In the absence of a variety of flowering shrubs, effects with water were especially important and every effort was expended to make them as varied and unusual as possible. At Vaux, Le Nôtre began the clever use of water which was to become increasingly intricate as time went on. At one point there was a grille composed of slender spouts of water on either side of the center axis; spouts of water rose to form medium-high walls of crystal between which the guests, in their satin garments and hats trimmed with ostrich feathers, walked without becoming wet. The spouts fell into square basins bordered with grass, and the basins were connected by rivulets.

In a garden, as in a play or a symphony, the author builds up to his great climax through lesser ones. At Vaux, among the lesser climaxes was a series of cascades located on the bank which supported the last terrace facing the canal. The waters tumbled from masks and shells, set in a long wall built of colored stones, into a pool separated from the canal by a broad, graveled terrace. Since the bank was not visible from the house, the cascades could not be seen until one reached them; yet their tumbling and splashing resounded throughout the gardens, constituting a gradual crescendo as one approached. A second minor climax, also not seen until the visitor was upon it, was the canal called La Poèle (actually the river Anqueuil), which was straightened out and made to flow between banks of marble for half a mile inside the park.

Beyond the canal was the final climax, the grotto, designed by Le Nôtre and characterized, like much of his work, by large rough-surfaced stones. There was no surprise here for the grotto was raised so that it could be seen from every part of the park. Actually it was a sandstone wall, with seven shell-shaped niches supporting the terrace above it. In the niches were half-recumbent figures executed by the sculptor Mathieu Lespagnandel, representing the rivers Tiber and Anqueuil. Lack of time had prevented the execution of a fine bridge across the canal, so the guests crossed on a temporary one of wood. Stairways led to terraces above and behind the grotto, and past other features to the statue of Hercules.

The King walked the two miles to the statue. Le Nôtre knew how much he wanted to be a successful king, the actual ruler of France; he realized how Louis must have felt when confronted with the brilliant accomplishments of this minister who always treated him as *le pauvre petit*—the poor unfortunate boy of the Fronde. So Le Nôtre said to him, "*Votre Majesté a de grandeur d'esprit.*"

As they stood there, once again the garden was spread before them in its entirety, this time looking toward the cream-colored house flanked by red service buildings with blue roofs, which together were like a backdrop to a stage set. The unity of the scheme was emphasized by having on the house a dome of the same shape as the amphitheatre above the grotto.

Turning to Fouquet, the King said, "I am surprised." The minister thought the King meant surprise at the beauty of the house and park; insensitive to the tone of voice which expressed displeasure with his daring and extravagance, he answered with his customary aplomb, "Sire, I am surprised at your surprise."

After the garden walk, a superlative entertainment followed. Its program, amplified, was to be repeated many times at Versailles. There was a feast out-of-doors. A poem by Paul Pellisson was recited by the popular actress La Béjart. A play by Molière, *L'avertissement des facheaux*, interspersed with ballets, was presented by him and his company. Lastly there were fireworks that lit up the garden.

The party was described by various authors, among them La Fontaine in his poem, *Le songe de vaux*, and the novelist Mademoiselle de Scudéry, close friend of the writer, Paul Pellisson, who worked for Fouquet. Pellisson wrote a response, apparently to be recited by Le Nôtre, reproving François de Bois-Robert, whose poem had omitted many details about the garden:

Où sont dans vos beaux vers mes buis et mes gazons
Taillés en tant de façons?
Que vous a fait ma superbe Couronne
Qui prétend, sans façonner,
Bien mériter qu'on se donne
Le soin de la couronner?

En bonne foi, vous devait-il suffire
D'avoir nommé dans vos vers les plus beaux
    Ce que vous pouviez décrire
Et que je sais mieux ordonner que dire:
Nos prés, nos bois, nos sources, nos canaux,
Nos grands vergers, nos longues palissades,
Nos larges mers, nos torrents, nos cascades.
Non: il fallait d'un plus hardi dessein
Sur chaque object porter cent fois la main,
Ronger ses doigts, s'échauffer la cervelle
Pour peindre au vif une chose si belle.

Three short weeks after the fête, given ostensibly in the King's honor, Fouquet was arrested by the Mousquetaire d'Artagnan (much later a hero of Dumas' novels) and cast into jail. Immediately all work stopped at Vaux, all employees but a handful of personal servants were dismissed, and the great castle with its park was left as deserted as the palace of Sleeping Beauty after the spell had been cast upon her.

Fouquet's trial lasted for three years and kept France buzzing with discussion. Many then thought—as many still do today—that he was treated too severely, since he was no more dishonest than his predecessors, who had also become rich by selling offices and farming out taxes. However, some time before Fouquet's arrest, Colbert and the King had given him a chance to reform. When, after seven months of honesty, he again lapsed into his old ways they made him believe he was to be *premier ministre* and induced him to sell his parliamentary position of *procureur général* so he would not have to be tried by his equals. They persuaded him to hand over to the King the 1,4000,000 *livres* that was paid for it. In a state centered round the King there was no room for a man like Fouquet.

He was so gifted, had so many powerful friends, and sentiment in his favor was so strong, that at the end of this trial he was imprisoned instead of being put to death as the King had intended. By the time he was liberated, his spirit had been broken and he died soon after, in 1680.

Today, the château and its gardens are almost as they were when Louis XIV and his court came there in 1661. The place has been restored and refurnished, first under the ownership of Alfred Sommier, who began the work in 1875, engaging M. Laine to do the gardens. Later, Edmé Sommier carried on, employing the landscape architect M. Duchêne. They worked from old plans, from Silvestre's engravings, and other contemporary prints and documents.

In Fouquet's time, Charles Perrault was a frequent guest at Vaux; to the present-day visitor the château and its park are so unreal in their perfection that they appear like a setting for one of his fairy tales. In the gardens, seen on a late summer afternoon with the sun slanting across the empty *allées* and lighting the fountains, the memory of Fouquet's sudden eclipse is still vivid, pervading the place with a sense of ominous drama.

Le Nôtre never expressed in writing his ideas about garden planning. His style has to be studied from plans and from the gardens themselves. One of his pupils Alexander Le Blond (under the name of Dezalliers d'Argenville) wrote a book in 1739, *La theorie et la pratique du jardinage*, in which he stated the principles that governed Le Nôtre's work. In garden design these rules are what grammar is to speech or scales to music. They apply to all gardens, large and small, from Persia to the suburbs of New York or San Francisco. When there is something wrong about a garden it can generally be traced to failure to comply with one or more of these rules.

The rules are: the garden must be in harmony with the conformation of the land, that is, in accord with the situation whether it is in the mountains, on the seashore or in a desert such as the American Southwest; it must be planned for the climate, in terms of whether it is hot or cold, damp or dry, or combinations of these; it must form a unit with the house, harmonizing with its proportions as well as its size and style; and lastly it must be appropriate to the owner's pocketbook, his way of life and tastes.

Le Blond set down other rules: Do not, he continued, darken the garden too much, and do not have too much growth close to the house,

Vaux-le-Vicomte. Detail of the garden.

but do keep a space open for fine views; on the other hand, do not open them too much. He advised making a garden appear always larger than it is, but not to make it too open for then it is likely to merge into the countryside and seem smaller than it actually is. Still other rules, which obviously were followed in Le Nôtre's work, include the advice that the garden should be one-third longer than wide, and that one feature should always be balanced by another, such as a wood by a parterre. There should be variety, and no designs in the beds should be repeated. Statues should look inevitable, canals should be used in low places, and woods should be planted on the sides and at the back of the house. Moreover, planting should be done in terms of how it would

Vaux-le-Vicomte. View from the château.

look twenty years later, so that the whole would not have to be changed after the trees had grown.

In the typical scheme of a classical garden, a central axis led from the main door of the house and divided the garden in two. Along this axis were lawns and watercourses. Crossing it would be lesser lateral axes which divided the garden into a series of parterres, often on different levels, preferably stepped, one below the next to emphasize the house; the latter should, of course, be set high in order to dominate the scene. Round the house would be wide spaces so the sun could shine in on all sides. There would be no foundation planting of shrubs because these might cause shade, be damp or, with the memory of the fortress in mind, provide a place for enemies to lurk. The parterres on the terraces close to the house would be planted in highly complicated patterns, generally of embroidery, and parterres farther away would be simpler, until the last, nearest the woods, would be *à l'Anglaise*, that is, of turf.

Le Nôtre used the rules so well that his gardens appeared to grow out of the soil and looked as if no other solution was possible. Much of his work was intended for people who wanted to impress the world with their wealth and taste by entertaining on a lavish scale. For them he built out-of-door drawing-rooms and concert halls. For other kinds of clients, such as Madame de Sévigné, who lived quietly at her estate, les Rochers, in Brittany, there was a poetic wood. At Meaux he made a shaded walk for meditation and at the Trianon a gay flower garden for relaxation. He enclosed his town gardens with high trellises for privacy, and in the royal parks, which are now public, he made paths wide enough to support heavy traffic.

In his plans he used features that were already traditional in French gardens and that had developed during the years when the château with its park was growing out of the fortified castle. Thus the approaches were always in a series of courtyards which were a modernization of medieval baileys. He also followed the custom, already established in his time, of having the house stand between the approaches and the garden. Moreover, house and garden formed an indivisible unit and enhanced each other. On the garden side, paths seemed to originate from doors and windows while other features were placed to make pictures when viewed from certain rooms.

The plans were thought out to the least detail and outlined on paper before a spade touched the ground. Occasionally a scheme would be too expensive to be undertaken all at one time and had to be completed later, as at Ormesson and Sceaux. The King, the Prince de Condé and undoubtedly other great nobles liked to change their buildings and parks after they had been laid out but in the parks of Le Nôtre such changes were made only in details and not in the original scheme.

Le Nôtre's gardens were conceived as a painter composes a picture, except that his pictures were to be viewed from several approaches. These pictures were always framed by clipped hedges and, behind them, by high trees, both planted at the same time so as to mature together and so the stronger growth would not interfere with the weaker. Later the lower branches would be cut off and the upper ones permitted to spread out over the hedges and cast a shadow to emphasize the frame with a strong, dark line.

There were few flowering shrubs and trees and no specimen plants in these gardens, so color was provided by water, sky, grass and statuary as well as by flowers. The flowers, however, were not allowed to spread out in shapes natural to them but were clipped and trained to form accents or notes of color. When the wind blew there was no swaying of branches on trees, shrubs or flowers. They were all too strictly trimmed for that. Action was furnished by spouting fountains and foaming cascades, by the slow changing of shadows cast on the graveled walks or level greenswards by marble statues or by clouds moving across the vast expanse of sky over the flatly planted terraces. Though the gardens were immense, they followed the idea of a *hortus inclusus*, that is, views from them, with some notable exceptions, did not take in the scenery outside the boundaries. This practice was based on the principle of keeping the garden from merging into the countryside. It also gave the owner the feeling, when he walked on his terraces, that he was master of all the land he could see.

After the gardens were finished, though there had been a vast upheaval of earth to accomplish the grading, the surfaces would be as smooth as marble in a sculptor's finished statue. When the flowers had been set in their beds and the water turned on, each line and curve of the original plan would be clear and no detail blurred or crowded. Art, not nature, was supreme in these gardens and every tree, rosebush, althea or pyracantha, annual or perennial was clipped, pinched back or otherwise disciplined to conform to a preconceived pattern. No branch was allowed to grow out too far nor chance seedling to reach maturity. Today such exactitude in the shapes of plant material is not admired but in Le Nôtre's time, when nature was fearsome, this complete domination over it was regarded as evidence of man's dexterity and strength of purpose.

Often when a lesser artist laid out a classical garden, the effect was stiff and dry. But Le Nôtre had such a remarkable sense of proportion in the use of masses, spaces and perspectives, such a genius for eliminating unnecessary details, that the effect of one of his gardens was like that of a Bach chorale, where all voices interweave to make a rich, harmonious whole.

CHAPTER VII

VERSAILLES

GROWING STEADILY, LE NÔTRE, by 1661, was at the height of his ability as an artist and of wit and verve as a person. He gloried to create superlative parks and gardens, and the year began a time of great activity for him. Besides his great work at Versailles, which was to continue for about thirty years, he was in charge of additions and reconstructions at the Louvre, the Tuileries and Fontainebleau; he also went to England to make plans for Charles II, and had commissions for private clients.

Most contemporaries thought the idea underlying the creation of Versailles was to magnify the King's honor and glory, two words frequently on their tongues. But Colbert, the King and Le Nôtre knew that Versailles was also a vast scheme to make France pre-eminent. The succession of new buildings and gardens, as well as fantastic parties, provided subjects for writers and for conversation. They were intended to keep the wealth, talent and power of the country before France and the world, and to instill fear and respect in the minds of friends and enemies.

The King's choice of Versailles for his great palace and park, instead of far more attractive sites in the countryside of France, aroused much unfavorable criticism. Colbert objected because he thought the King should live among his people in Paris, that he should embellish the Louvre and make it, his principal residence, rather than a remote country estate. Colbert wanted to keep the exchequer balanced and was appalled at the expense of transforming an unhealthy, swampy site, which had no view and almost no water, into an estate suitable for a royal residence. He wrote to Louis that Le Nôtre and

Le Vau "knew the King practically only at Versailles, that is, amid pleasures and diversions . . . If His Majesty is not warned against them, it will result in their leading him from one project to another in the hopes of rendering these works immortal."

Colbert's warnings were not heeded. Within two years after the work had begun at Versailles, 1,500,000 *livres* had been spent merely to fill in the terrace in front of the château. Perhaps the very difficulties of the site was one of the reasons Versailles appealed to the King. Here where nature had been so niggardly, was an opportunity to create a park and palace springing entirely from the minds of his artists and the hands of his artisans.

At Versailles, Louis XIII had built a charming hunting-lodge of rose-colored brick with white stone coigns and a sloping roof covered with black slate. Situated on an elevation, it had at one side a little garden designed by Boyceau and also a tennis court. Louis XIV liked the house so much he kept it, though much changed, in the heart of his great white marble palace.

From Vaux, Louis brought to Versailles all the architects, painters and sculptors and most of the craftsmen who had worked at Maincy, near by, making furniture and textiles for Fouquet's house. He even had five hundred orange trees and other plants brought from the nurseries at Vaux. All this was before Fouquet had been sentenced.

Almost from the beginning, the King and Le Nôtre planned to create outside the park a town which was to become the capital of France, though this did not come to pass for twenty years. The plan was credited to Mansart, but Le Nôtre undoubtedly had a hand in it. The town, château and garden are so united that it is possible to use the walks in the park to go from one part of the town to another.

When streets were laid out and building sites measured off, Le Nôtre bought one and built himself a fine house, and so did Charles Perrault and Jean de La Quintinie. Le Nôtre's house, located at number 18 of the present rue Hoche, was next door to that of Pierre de Francine, his collaborator and the King's fountaineer. Later, when houses were in demand, Le Nôtre sold his for 270,000 *livres*.

To provide for the expected traffic, three roads were laid out fanwise from the approach, with a square, called *Place d'Armes*, situated outside the first courtyard of the castle. The *Place d'Armes* was so huge that Louis could review a whole army in it, which he delighted to do, showing off to the ladies of the court who formed a fluttery, flirting bevy behind him.

At Versailles, Le Nôtre and the King were as one; they agreed entirely. In his *Memoires* the King wrote that he did not wish to create but to "understand everything." He had great esteem for the men of genius with whom he had surrounded himself. He enjoyed the bustle associated with building; and he liked to watch a room being painted and to supervise the moving and placing of furniture. He would take a pair of shears from the gardener to clip a hedge, and he would turn on spigots to open pipes for his fountains. He did not mind dodging excavations, becoming covered with dust, or muddying his shoes while visiting the park to inspect new constructions. In short, like his predecessors, the Valois kings, Louis had a great love for building. On walks through the park with Le Nôtre beside him, he would inspect and criticize fountains, trellises and vistas with a view to improving them. It gave him pleasure to exercise his fine taste and sense of proportion; for example, the King and his gardener, with Le Brun and perhaps Le Vau, would decide to move a hill in order to widen a view or they would change the tops of the windows in the *Galerie des Glaces* from square to round.

On a sunny day in the year 1662, soon after work had started at Versailles, a cavalcade escorted by a troop of cavalry, drummers and trumpeters rumbled down the dusty road. The gaily painted coaches, each drawn by six horses with outriders, were occupied by Louis' wife and mother and ladies-in-waiting. They were accompanied by young cavaliers on horse-back, among them the King; as they clattered up to the entrance they were met, as was the custom, by the rolling of drums and blare of trumpets, by ministers and valets waiting in front of a double row of guards that formed a human hedge. The young King dismounted gracefully and was greeted by Colbert, Le Nôtre, Le Vau and others working at the château. All but Le Nôtre bowed low, but he, as was his wont when the King returned from a journey, embraced him, kissing him on both cheeks with a combination of respect, love and enthusiasm.

There is a story of another such informal meeting when the design for the *Petit Parc*, the heart of the later vast park, had been completed. The King and Le Nôtre, who carried a roll of plans under his arm, followed

Overleaf: Versailles. View of the château, gardens and town.

by ministers, contractors and architects, stepped through scaffolding and around ladders set up in the château, then out onto the mound which was to be the first parterre. A plank was placed across two horses to provide a table, and there Le Nôtre spread out the first of his plans. The King looked at it, was pleased and said, "Le Nôtre, for this I will give you twenty thousand *livres*." Le Nôtre thanked the King and spread out his second plan. The King, delighted, called to the others in the group to look; turning to Le Nôtre he said, "I will give you twenty thousand *livres* for this one too." Again Le Nôtre bowed and thanked the King. By this time he was flushed with pleasure and eagerly unrolled the third of his drawings. The King threw up his hands and said, "Le Nôtre, it is magnificent, I must give you another twenty thousand *livres*." After being thanked again, the King waited for more plans to be unrolled, but Le Nôtre put his hands over the remaining drawings. With a twinkle in his blue eyes, he said, "Sire, you will not see any more for otherwise I should ruin you."

The palace at Versailles was changed three times in the seventeenth century, twice by Le Vau and then radically by Mansart; and other alterations were made later, so there is not the same unity between castle and park as in other classical designs. However, in the park itself there is that same relation of one part to the others and of subordination of details to the whole that is typical of all of Le Nôtre's work. The original plan, called the *Petit Parc*, followed the three fundamental rules of garden design so faithfully that it was never changed, only greatly enlarged from the original dimensions. The plan was suited to the lie of the land, which had a slight slope toward the west. There were broad terraces to catch the sun during damp, cool winter months; shaded woods with splashing fountains for the sake of coolness on hot summer days; and out-of-door ballrooms and concert halls to provide a setting for entertainment, while dramatic stairways furnished backgrounds for the pageant-like parties.

The château is approached by three courtyards in the traditional French way. Like everything else at Versailles they are immense. The first courtyard led to the second through a pair of exquisitely wrought iron gates that came from the château of Maisons. This second courtyard was flanked at the time by two wings. Opposite the south wing was a building called the *Grand Commun*, which was situated on the rue de la Surintendence: here Le Nôtre at first (and also later in life) had an apartment, as did other artists

Versailles. View of the Orangerie. By Rigaud.

and officials in the king's service. From this court the way led to a third and innermost court, the *Cour de Marbre* in front of the facade of Louis XIII's transformed hunting lodge. At times a temporary theatre would be set up there and a play by Molière or an opera by Lulli would be performed for the courtiers as part of an evening's entertainment. Besides the play, the pleasure-loving aristocrats would enjoy a collation, a drive through the park, a row on a lake, perhaps a ball in one of the bosquets and a few hours of gambling at cards—all in one evening!

Louis surfeited his nobles with pleasure, encouraged them to gamble and kept them away from their estates—all to lessen their power and wealth, so they could no longer be a threat to him.

After the first plans had been executed, praise was showered on Le Nôtre but he was not satisfied with his work. When he took Bernini, the famous Italian architect and sculptor around the park, he told him it was barely sketched out and the whole was too narrow.

The park had three vistas, the main one extending to the west and the lesser ones north and south. Each began at a parterre directly in front of the palace or its wings. To the west the great central vista, perhaps the most dramatic in any garden, began at the parterre beneath the *Galerie des Glaces*, where treaties for both victories and defeats have since been signed by France. The decoration for this parterre had originally been a pattern carried out in box; it was then changed to five pools, similar to but not so attractive as the water parterre at Chantilly; and in the final stage there were two great pools in an exceedingly simple and effective treatment. These pools are immense; and along their rims are groups of statuary, representing the rivers of France, alternating with nymphs.

From the first terrace the vista crosses the parterre of Latona, which is reached from the upper level by a horseshoe-shaped stairway. The statuary representing the story of Latona is surrounded by colorful flower borders. Thence the vista continues along a rectangular green panel called at that time the *Allée Royale*; later, when kings were in disfavor, this area was called the *Tapis Vert*. The vista is framed by rows of trees and behind them on either side of the *Tapis Vert* are the room-like gardens called *bosquets*.

At first Le Nôtre placed trellises to serve as a frame under the trees and covered them with ivy or jasmine to obtain the effect of a hedge. Later he planted hedges of hornbeam called *charmilles*, with oaks and elms behind them. Marble statues and huge vases, on pedestals, were placed in front of the clipped green hedges. They provided white accents and gave stability to the *allée* which, because of perspective, appeared to rise. Beyond the green panel there was a space, like a period after a sentence, then came a round pool first called *Bassin des Cygnes* and later *Bassin d'Appollon*, from three groups of statues (which had been moved several times). The central and largest group represented Apollo—symbol of Louis—the sun god, back from his daily trip across the skies, being received by Thetis and her nymphs; in the lesser groups his horses are being groomed by Tritons. When one looks back from this point the château appears high up and is framed by the green walls of the *allée*.

From its inception, Le Nôtre had planned to continue the axis beyond the *bassin* toward the horizon but until this could be accomplished

Versailles. View of the Orangerie.

82

the intended lines were indicated by avenues of trees. When the axis was built out it led to a high waterspout, a place to rest the eye before it went on to the head of the Grand Canal. The canal itself was enormous, almost a mile long and three hundred sixty feet wide; it was perhaps the greatest of all Le Nôtre's conquests over nature for he planned it despite the absence of sufficient water. The severity of the lines of the canal was broken by widening at three places. One-third the way down was a transverse axis of water in the shape of a secondary canal which, at its northern end, met the stairways and terraces of the *Grand Trianon*, first built in 1668; at its southern end was the menagerie.

On this tremendous body of artificial water were many boats. Here it was customary to try out a new model for a warship. The Venetians sent gondolas as gifts to the King, and the intention was to have boats from all nations. The guests stepped into the boats and were rowed along, some of them from late at night until dawn, followed by other boats filled with musicians. During fête nights the lights of myriad candles and torches glinted on the waters and on the jewels and satins of the courtiers.

At the time, poets said the vista formed a pathway to the heavens so that the sun god, father of life, could descend to his domain at Versailles. To Le Nôtre and Colbert the great view merging with the horizon expressed the limitless power of the King, who personified France.

Louis could hardly wait for the first extensions to the château and the first sections of the park to be finished to give a spectacular fête, which was to outshine Fouquet's by far. It took place in May 1664 and lasted a week and was called *Les plaisirs de l'île enchantée*. The program was written by Molière. The hero was Roger, impersonated by the King, who was an expert and graceful actor and dancer. At night during this fête and later at others, marvellous effects were obtained by lights. Some outlined fountains and canals; in the *bosquets* huge chandeliers were hung to light up the audience; and other lights were suspended behind trees. The garden where guests partook of supper was lighted with torches held by *laquais* in splendid uniforms. In front of the château, Roman candles were set off for color effects.

To the south of the château was the second series of terraces. Though it was rebuilt each time the house was enlarged, the underlying concept remained unchanged. In its final form it begins at the parterre called *du Midi*, which is embellished with box-edged beds filled with flowers. This

Versailles. The Fountain of Loatna.

parterre rests on the *orangerie* under it and the balustrade which bounds it is also on top of the roof of the building below. The present *orangerie* is the second one to be built. The design was by Le Nôtre though it has always been attributed to Mansart, who carried it out. It is simple, suited to its purpose and fits perfectly into the slope of the land. The stone work has the strong horizontal lines characteristic of Le Nôtre's other architectural work. The whole building is four hundred fifty feet long. It is protected from the north by the bank of terraces and faces south where high windows, rounded

Versailles. Illumination of the palace and gardens during a fête.
An engraving by Le Pautre.

at the top, get the full benefit of the sun. In the center, four pairs of double
columns with capitals support the entablature. The corners are rounded and
abut the two wings, which protect the building and garden from east and
west winds. In these wings are the stairways—considered among the finest
ever built out-of-doors. They descend from the level above to the garden in
front of the building, and have one hundred and three steps with low risers.
They terminate in wrought-iron grilles hung from imposing gate posts.

To line the roof of the *orangerie*, and make it waterproof and warm, Le Nôtre used linen covered with plaster.

In front of the building is a charming garden where beds of turf and fountains provide a setting for tubs holding trees laden with oranges and other yellow citrus fruits or reddish pomegranates, bushes of white cape jasmine, and pink-and-red-flowered oleanders. The plants in their tubs were wheeled out in spring, each to its allotted place, to form part of the planned pattern in the garden, and back again in the autumn on barrows, which in the heyday of Versailles were made of silver. Among the orange trees was a famous old one called the *Grand Bourbon*, brought from Fontainebleau, and said to have been planted originally in 1421. It is still alive; if it is as old as tradition claims, it is a remarkable proof of the continuity of the horticultural skill of French gardeners.

Beyond the *orangerie*, the western vista led across a road which went to Saint-Cyr, where Madame de Maintenon had her school for impoverished young noblewomen, which she visited almost every day. On the other side of the road was the *Lac des Suisses* visible from the terrace above. This lake was Le Nôtre's last work at Versailles, completed when he was seventy-seven years old. Here two schooners were moored, gay with blue and white pennants fluttering from their masts. Fanciful costumes were worn by the sailors who manned them.

The land here was swampy; it was held responsible for the bad air, then considered to be the cause of malaria. Tremendous amounts of earth, excavated for the lake, were carried to an adjoining plot to raise the land for the King's vegetable garden, laid out under the direction of Jean de La Quintinie. To do this work a regiment of Swiss Guards, like forced labor, was brought in; hundreds of the men died of malaria and were carried away in carts at night so as not to frighten the other workmen, according to Madame de Sévigné, who records this ghastly fact without any sign of being disturbed by it.

North of the château, where the ground sloped sharply, is the third vista, and the last part of the park to be developed. The parterre nearest the wing of the château called *du Nord*, remains almost exactly as shown in the contemporary painting by Allegrain. Like the main vista it is framed by hedges and trees and has marble statues in front of the green walls. In masking the slope, Le Nôtre showed his complete mastery of perspectives for he made the beds wedge-shaped, with distant beds shorter and smaller and near ones larger, and with the longest side of the triangles facing the château. In the center of this parterre was the Fountain of the Pyramid by Girardon. Steps of rose-colored marble (celebrated by the poets of the day) led from the terrace to the parterre. They had risers low in proportion to the treads, thus compelling visitors to descend slowly and take in the scene in a leisurely fashion. Byeond the parterre was the *Allée des Marmousets*, which was a most poetic rendering of a steep avenue leading down a hill through a wood. The two rows of fountains which decorate it were designed by Charles Perrault. Each was composed of three children, girls and boys (the marmousets), who hold a basin from which water rises in high spouts. At the lowest extremity of the *allée* is the great basin called *du Dragon* and beyond it is another and larger one called *de Neptune* and noted for its graceful shape. The vista beyond this basin was unique at Versailles for it ended in a grille through which the distant countryside could be glimpsed.

The *allée* was opened in September 1670 with a great fête; it was filled with potted plants, and refreshments were served from silver platters newly come from the Gobelins. In one bower-like tent erected for the occasion were fruit trees in tubs, with pears, currants, apricots and cherries suspended from their branches and ready to be plucked and eaten.

To modern visitors, as also to the painters of the eighteenth century such as Watteau, Lancret and Boucher, the woods at Versailles on either side of the *Allée Royale* between the parterre of Latona and the cross-axis at right angles to the head of the canal, are the most appealing places in the park. There is no undergrowth in the woods of Le Nôtre, except for an occasional ground cover of ivy or Vinca, so the trunks of the trees, which are evenly spaced, are clearly seen and frequently the sides facing north are emerald green from moss growing on them. The width of the sanded paths leading through these woods is in perfect proportion to the height of the trees, which are naturally low-growing. Moreover, with his painter's eye Le Nôtre made them wide enough for the sun to shine across them in slanting rays and brighten groups of statuary or marble benches or perhaps even cast light on the water bubbling from a pool and causing it to sparkle.

In striking contrast to the sobriety of these woods were the bosquets serving as *al fresco* ballrooms, theatres or concert halls. They were begun at the height of Louis' power and flowered during the sway of Madame

Versailles. Parterre du Nord as seen from the château.

de Montespan, which began in 1668 and lasted ten years, her fall coinciding with the final subjugation of Franche Comté. The *bosquets* were an expression in permanent materials of the temporary bowers which had been erected for the fêtes. Some of them, big enough to seat three thousand spectators, had been designed and decorated by the finest artists at Versailles. Elaborate systems of pipes had been laid to carry water into them to play the fountains. Statues were brought from other parts of the park along with plants in tubs and pots as well as tapestries from the palace; and garlands of flowers were festooned wherever they would be effective. They were decorated with an eye to effects at night, when lights would glimmer and sparkle on crystal balls and chandeliers, silver vases and gauze scarves.

The first *bosquet* was the *Salle de Festin* or *du Conseil*, later replaced by the *Fontaine de l'Obélisque*. It was a glade with an isle in the center surrounded by a canal. To play practical jokes on guests, there were movable bridges that could be drawn up unexpectedly and thus left the promenader marooned on an island. In the *bosquet* called *Montagne d'Eau* and later the *Étoile*, the general effect consisted of five waterfalls round a basin from which five *allées* radiated. Each *allée* was bordered with a trellis covered with a hedge of honeysuckle. Along the top of it stood porcelain pots filled with flowers. The trellis had niches, each with a jet of water. At the base of the trellis ran a canal, its border of turf, its margins studded with shells. In the center was a rock and from the heart of it rose a huge spout of water which was surrounded by eight smaller ones combining to form a liquid mountain.

The *théâtre* or *amphithéâtre d'Eau*, situated north of the parterre of Latona and west of the *Allée des Marmousets*, was first opened to the court on the fourth day of the fête of 1674. Like many of these "secret gardens" it was circular and divided into two parts. The higher part was the stage, which was reached by steps and had falling water at the center. There was a grassy slope at the back of the stage from which three *allées* led out to form three vistas to the woods surrounding the *bosquet*. The lower part was semicircular and corresponded to the orchestra in a theatre. Three steps formed the seats and behind them was a *palissade* of sheared hornbeam.

Other decorations, odd to modern eyes, were marble consoles, buffets, pitchers and dishes made to simulate real vessels. In all these *bosquets* there was not a flat or smooth surface except for the turf underfoot, and even that was stepped and interrupted by canals lined with shells. Walls were of trelliswork made as complicated as possible. Jets of water formed arbors, waterfalls, aigrettes and fleur-de-lis and were contrived so that guests could sit amid them without getting wet. In one *bosquet* cascades of water fell over steps through which lights shone, and above this sat the orchestra—a damp situation hardly suited to the stringed instruments.

It is difficult to understand why Le Nôtre, who knew so well how to leave out the superfluous, who designed wide surfaces of water and level greenswards which produced an effect of calm and majesty, created

Versailles. The Fountain of Apollo, looking toward the château.

these overornamented *bosquets*. Perhaps he was carried away by the enthusiasm or ideas of others, or by the overwhelming fertility of his own imagination. He was close enough to the King to realize how difficult it was becoming to surprise the surfeited court as well as the world outside with novelties. The redundant ornamentation in these out-of-door ballrooms became the fashion and was carried out at Chantilly, Saint-Cloud and other parks. However, the proportions of the skeletal plans were so right that now, when most of the ornaments have been removed, the so-called "secret gardens" are charming.

While the *bosquets* were being designed, they naturally occasioned much comment; everyone who could do so tried to think up new ideas for them. There were the *Bosquet des Dômes* with marble balustrades; the two charming pavilions of the *Salle de Bal*; the *bosquet* of the giant; and the one of the Arc de Triompe. Madame de Montespan had an idea for a *bosquet:* a bronze tree with leaves of tin surrounded by metal reeds with the water spouting from all the leaves as well as the reeds. The idea was so absurd that Le Nôtre is said to have shrugged his shoulders and refused to have anything to do with it. Colbert, seeing how eager the King was to please his mistress, attended to all the details himself. But this creation soon vanished.

When the days of economy came to Versailles along with military reverses and a realization that debts had to be paid and money provided for needs other than pleasures and palaces, many of the *bosquets* were abandoned and others simplified, and have remained so to this day.

Unfortunately the most charming and most original of all the *bosquets* has disappeared entirely. It was a maze, a witty, original handling of an old theme. Mazes have long been popular as delightful places in which to flirt, play tag or get lost. At Versailles the maze was a place where lovers parted at dawn and where later in the morning Fénelon would walk with the young Dauphin whom he was tutoring to be a righteous king. It was designed at the time when the first volume of La Fontaine's version of Aesop's fables had appeared and children all over France were reciting them—as they still do today. Le Nôtre, who knew La Fontaine well, used the characters to embellish his maze, putting a statue of the Greek dwarf on one side of the entrance and Cupid holding Ariadne's string on the other. Instead of making the paths geometrical, Le Nôtre made them irregular, and occasionally curving. Where two met he placed a little exedra of trelliswork with a *bassin* and rockery or a fountain. In each exedra there was a group of painted lead figures representing the fox and grapes, the swan and goose, the wolf and the goose, or other characters from the *Fables*, executed in lifelike fashion. These figures were meant to make the visitor stop, look, and forget his way.

Le Nôtre worked at Versailles until he was seventy-seven years old; then he relinquished his place to Mansart and others though he continued to be superintendant of the buildings. In all his work here, he managed never to antagonize any of his colleagues or any of the courtiers. He walked through the forest of intrigue, where reputations was as fragile as

Louis XIV, Le Nôtre and members of the court making a tour of the Parterre du Nord at Versailles. A painting by Allegrain.

leaves about to fall, with his plans in his hands and tongue in cheek. He was honest and sincere and so able that he was respected and liked by everyone. All admired his work and felt that its glory increased the prestige of France. Though he was well aware of his genius, his achievements never went to his head: throughout, he maintained the attitude of the King's faithful servant. He could do this because he really felt that way.

CHAPTER VIII

THE WORKSHOP
AT VERSAILLES

THERE IS A SAYING that "the beauties of Versailles flow in the blood of the French people." Versailles epitomizes their genius. To bring forth this national masterpiece, the best talents in France were called upon. It is to Louis' credit that with few exceptions every contemporary Frenchman of talent or genius—architects, gardeners, engineers, poets, dramatists, musicians, and actors—contributed to Versailles or its fêtes. From 1661, when work was begun, until shortly after 1682, when Versailles became the political capital of France, it replaced Anet and Vaux as the artistic center of the country. Every phase of life, contemporary and historical, actual and mythological, contributed to ornament the palace and its park.

Moreover, such high standards of accomplishment were held up to the French people that they have been leaders in the arts from that day to this. They love Versailles not only because of its splendor and beauty but because of its place in their history, and thousands of them throng to it on holidays and on those Sundays when the waters of the fountains are turned on.

The creation of a national work of art on the scale of Versailles required an incredible amount of planning. Both Colbert and Louis XIV were equal to the task. Colbert organized all the arts into a hierarchy. There were three *contrôleurs généraux* and three *surintendants des bâtiments*. Among

Marche du Roy, et de ses cheualiers, auec toutes
leurs suittes, au tour du Camp de la course de

Premiere Journée.

bague, representant Roger, et les autres Cheualiers
enchantez, dans l'Isle d'Alcine

Versailles. Pageant of *Les Plaisirs de l'Isle Enchantée*. An engraving by Silvestre.

the latter was Le Nôtre, who held the office from 1657 until 1698, when he handed it on to his two nephews, Claude Desgots and Jean Michel Le Bouteux. His colleagues were Sieur Le Febre and Le Vau, and from 1672 Charles Perrault. When Le Vau died in 1678 he was succeeded by Mansart. Over them all was Colbert, to whom everything was shown in detail. He in turn reported to the King. Even when the King was at war, a model was made and sent to him along with written descriptions which he would return with marginal notes.

Bontemps was governor of Versailles. Artists and artisans functioned under his jurisdiction. The King liked him, and he was a close friend of Le Nôtre. However, once the King had approved of a project in the park, Le Nôtre took all responsibility.

Le Brun was chief designer and head of the Gobelins, where household furnishings, which are still world famous, were manufactured, among them Aubusson rugs, bronze stair-rails and hardware, silver, furniture, and tapestries that to this day hang on the walls of the palaces. Articles were made from designs furnished by Le Brun and his assistants, eminent among whom were Le Pautre and Claude Perrault. They also made designs for palace interiors, statuary for the parks, decorations for the fêtes, and even trappings for elaborate royal funerals. The group functioned together so continuously that they achieved the extraordinary unity which prevails at Versailles: the same flourishes, curves and volutes, superimposed on a strong base, shaped every object from the fountains in the park to the key which opened the door to Madame de Montespan's bedroom. As time went on and the artists became more deft, they developed a lighter touch. Carried away by enthusiasm, they also increased the amount of ornament in a given space.

Like Le Nôtre, Le Brun used his art to enhance the King's glory. His work was virile, full of action and well suited for decorating palaces and gardens where everyone strove to be gay—perhaps to counteract the prevailing sense of insecurity in a milieu where the career of every courtier, artist and servant depended entirely on the King's favor. Though some of his colleagues regarded Le Brun more as a decorator-craftsman than as a painter, he and Le Nôtre apparently had a high regard for each other's work. Le Nôtre bought Le Brun's paintings for his collection and in turn Le Brun called in Le Nôtre to lay out his garden. The painter had studied with Vouet and then gone to Rome with Poussin. There he made drawings from antique models and studied Italian baroque art. As happens so frequently to those who wield power for a long time, he became autocratic; with age, he grew jealous of other painters and in time became unpopular. Three years before his retirement he wrote a petulant letter to Charles Errard, head of the French Academy in Rome, complaining that Le Nôtre had not carried out his request that he visit two Italian painters in regard to a matter of pensions from the French king. Le Nôtre had done so but had reported his findings to Colbert, not to Le Brun; he seems to have ignored the complaint.

Versailles. Parterre du Sud.

When work was begun at Versailles, the park appears to have been of primary interest to the King. In 1663, Colbert noted that during the two previous years 1,500,000 *livres* had been spent there, mostly on the grounds. Le Sieur Petit, who held a position under Colbert, reported progress to him in a letter dated February 17, 1663 (quoted by Pierre de Nolhac in *La création de Versailles*): "We have eighty-four men working on the terrace. We expect another brigade Monday . . . Three hundred are working valiantly at leveling at the orangerie."

Work did not proceed quickly enough to please Louis, so the number of workmen was increased, first to one thousand and then to fifteen hundred, all laboring under orders from Le Nôtre. Even then it was too slow; so a regiment, the first of many to be impressed, was called in, since they had no military duties at the time. They were evidently mercenaries, members of the Swiss Guard. After that, shocking as it seems today, entire regiments were engaged in the work. Even then Louis was dissatisfied with the progress; he went so far as to have the *curé* at Versailles grant the men a dispensation so they could work on Sundays and on fête days after mass. Indoors there were two shifts of carpenters, one working by night, the other by day. These extravagances were remembered by the French and helped build up their resentment against him.

A second army of men, working under the direction of Charles Le Brun, included such experts as mosaicists, inlayists, lapidaries, bronze founders, wood carvers, and painters. Artists and artisans were brought from all over Europe, and most of all from Italy.

Since all favors depended on the King or Colbert and, to a lesser degree, on Le Brun and the superintendents of buildings, there was a good deal of intrigue. Those who held office naturally wanted to secure them for their relatives after their death. Even Le Nôtre saw to it that some of his positions descended to his nephews. Competitions were held among designers for a projected plan and several contractors submitted bids, yet there was bribery. Despite the fact that Louis was an absolute monarch, there were difficulties with workmen: at one time a group constructing a wall refused to continue because of their working conditions and pay. Contractors had to be watched lest they use inferior or second-hand materials. A note in Le Nôtre's handwriting says of the roofing of two pavilions of the château, "*qu'on fournisse de bonne ardoise (tile) neuve,*" and again, "*qu'on place latte (lath) contre latte.*"

Besides superintending the buildings and designing parks, Le Nôtre in his capacity as a royal employee had to supervise the upkeep of the gardens. Before a fête it was his duty to see that all the paths were newly sanded and swept and the beds filled with fresh flowers. It appears odd that such an important individual should have so menial a job, but Le Nôtre and other even more exalted people such as Colbert were in the position of personal servants to the King, a relationship persisting from feudal times.

Versailles. The Fountains of Flora. An engraving by Le Pautre.

A seventeenth century garden without the foam, sparkle and glint of water was inconceivable. Rainbow-colored sprays blown out beyond the rims of fountains, wetting the rims and nearby paths seemed to fill the air with color, while ripples in ponds and large waves on the canals provided action and interest. But Louis, who could order engineers to level mountains and fill in swamps, who could change the whole countryside, found that he could not obtain water, because none was available. Despite the absence of

water, Le Nôtre continued to design elaborate fountains for the *bosquets*, great canals, and high spouts for the *allées*, all on a scale with the rest of Versailles. This called for an enormous supply of water. The King was so delighted with the plans that he urged Le Nôtre to continue with his drawings. Each encouraged the other, as though nothing stood in the way. Vauban, the great engineer, who was building fortresses around France, was called upon to help procure water. The Academy of Sciences and the mathematician Christian Huyghens were also consulted.

In a first attempt, the land nearby was tapped through underground drainage and all the moisture in the neighborhood drawn into a reservoir by means of pipes. These aqueducts and gutters were so well built that they are practically unchanged today. However, this supply proved insufficient; so in 1665 a pump and water tower were erected at great expense—later these were declared useless by Huyghens.

By 1666, after much effort, enough water had been secured to turn on the first fountains in the park. It was an exciting event for the King; in company with the fountaineers, the brothers de Francine, Colbert and of course Le Nôtre, he spent a goodly part of a day assisting in the adjustment of cocks and valves, not without becoming wet himself. Finally the water spurted into the air, at first a little muddied but soon forming myriads of crystal patterns as it rose from the basins and pools.

But much more water was needed. Remembering how Fouquet had changed the course of the river Anqueuil and made it run through his park, and how Le Grand Condé at Chantilly was using the river Nonette for some of his water effects, the King naturally turned to the rivers of France as a source of supply. The idea that fertile valleys might be dried up to play his fountains did not deter him. The first river to be tapped was the Seine but that did not furnish enough water. Before attempting to take water from another river, land farther away from the park was tapped and water brought by subterranean aqueducts that had been laboriously tunneled through many mountains.

For a time the river Bièvre was considered, then the Loire. Le Nôtre, in full agreement with the King about the water supply, is reported to have told him it might be a good idea to have boats descend from the Loire,

Versailles. The Fountains of Flora today.

be mounted on sledges to cross the hill of Satory to Versailles, and then be floated in on the grand canal. The King was highly enthusiastic about it, but both Colbert and Perrault realized the absurdity of such projects. They pretended to welcome all suggestions but the wily Colbert took great pains to prove each plan impracticable.

Of all the rivers they considered, the most feasible seemed to be the Eure, a tributary of the Seine that lay west of Versailles. Vauban approved of this project. In the agreement with the contractors it was specified that they could have as many troops for the work as they needed, the soldiers to be paid the equivalent of about ten cents a day. Work began in 1685. Outrageous as it appears to us today, thirty thousand soldiers labored night and day for three years. The King repeatedly inspected the work and reviewed the troops. Malaria was prevalent and many soldiers became ill and died. Louis took a preventive medicine, and escaped the malaria, but Louvois caught it. Meanwhile, the French armies had experienced reverses and the troops were required for active duty, so the work was halted. The King decided not to renew it. Over eight million *livres* and immense effort had been spent in vain.

There never has been enough water at Versailles; today the town still suffers from the lack of it. Courtiers of the seventeenth century received one small basinful for their daily ablutions. No wonder perfumes were popular! In the park, every drop has always been husbanded and used several times. Even in the days of Louis XIV the waters in the fountains were turned on only when the King was in residence, and then only from the time of the *levée* until evening. Except on special occasions they were restricted to the jets near the château, the basin of Neptune, and the fountains of the four seasons. The other waters were played only on days of entertainment. Today they are turned on one Sunday a month, and not all at one time but in succession. To see them it is necessary to walk quickly from one *bosquet* or *allée* to the next.

In a garden where the conformation of the land, the shapes of streams and lakes, and even the plant material, follow measurements made by rule and compass, man-made reproductions of nature such as statuary are surely appropriate. In such an architectural garden, statuary must harmonize with the balustrades and garden houses. Like the accurately lined-out paths and geometrically shaped waters, they are planned and designed to last for many centuries.

Statues brought life and interest in the seventeenth century gardens. In those days flowering trees such as magnolias, Japanese cherries, spiraeas, forsythias, rhododendrons, all the thousands of other woody and herbaceous plants which bring color, movement and variety of form to present-day gardens, were still growing, unknown to European gardeners, on the slopes of remote mountains in China, in the forests and swamps of North America, or in still undiscovered continents.

In order to produce the great number of statues needed for the park and palace, forty-six sculptors were employed in the workshops at Versailles. Though most of the statuary was original, there were also copies of antiques from sketches made by artists living at the French Academy in Rome, young men whom Colbert sent there to find objects worth buying and to make sketches of objects to be copied. Antiques were also brought from Gallo-Roman sources at Arles.

The subjects for original work were discussed at length by artists and by the King. The usual antagonism between classicists and modernists arose, so that the final decision was left to Academicians and they decreed in an entirely bureaucratic fashion what the statues were to represent. One collection was to consist of twenty allegorical groups, each to have six subgroups and these to consist of four elements, four seasons, four hours of the day, four parts of the world, four poems and four temperaments. Le Brun, Le Pautre and Perrault made sketches for these subjects. For some they used the characters who had taken part in the masks and plays produced by Molière and his troupe in *L'impromtu de Versailles*. The sculptors exercised much freedom in the execution of their statues while the greatest among them did not use the sketches at all.

As a result of this arbitrary way of creating works of art it is not surprising that some of the statuary should be banal, but most of it is charming and entirely suitable to the sylvan background in subject, scale and texture. There is a finesse, a delicacy and a gaiety in most of the pieces, even in copies from antique models. With few exceptions, gods and goddesses are not shown as heroic figures in fearsome or threatening attitudes, nor do they have agonized expressions. They are pleasing and graceful, their faces looking very much like those of the courtiers who intrigued and flirted in the park,

Versailles. The Fountain of Les Dômes. An engraving by Rigaud.

strolled in the *allées*, sat on the benches, read aloud to each other or were rowed on the canals.

The first sculpture at Versailles was made either of stone or a mixture of tin and lead which was gilded or painted with colors. Many of the earlier figures were later executed in marble or bronze. Colored lead proved so attractive that Le Nôtre used it for the figures representing Aesop's *Fables* in the *bosquet* of the maze.

To be effective, statues must be placed so the light strikes them without causing shadows that will change their expression. Moreover, as Le Blond wrote in his book on garden design, they must be an integral part of the scheme. In turn, the shrubbery or garden houses must form a frame or background for them. Le Nôtre excelled at placing statues; they always look as if they belong exactly where they are.

Among the particularly charming groups are the fountains of the four seasons, which are still situated at the crossing of *allées* that divide

Versailles. The Fountain of Les Dômes today.

the park (between the parterre of Latona and the arm of the canal) into four
large blocks of trees filled with bosquets. None of the symbols or ornaments
is particularly original but they are pleasing and some of them express
a playful spirit. In the open spaces cut out of the woods and outlined
by hedges of hornbeam are basins rimmed with white marble, in each of
which reclines a marble figure representing one of the seasons, accompanied by cherubs. From each center rises a high spurt of water. In the
fountain representing Spring, by Tuby, the principal figure is Flora and
is strewn with flowers. The fountain of Winter, by Girardon, shows
Saturn and is decorated with shells and icicles. One of the little cherubs in
the group is so cold he is creeping under the god's drapery for warmth.
Bacchus, by Marsy, represents Autumn. Huge bunches of grapes decorate
this fountain; instead of cherubs, baby fauns accompany the god. Ceres
by Regnaudin represents Summer, with decorations consisting of sheaves
of wheat.

Statues and paintings of children were everywhere at Versailles. They had been used in ancient times and again in Renaissance gardens. At Versailles they represented the fertility and virility of the Sun God, symbols intended to flatter the King.

Besides statuary there were vases and *termes* showing three-quarter length figures on pedestals. In a woodland garden near the parterre of Latona were fine *termes* executed from designs by Nicolas Poussin and originally intended for Vaux. Except for pairs, no two vases in the whole collection were alike. Some were copies, such as the two reproductions of the Medici and Borghese vases, but the majority were original in design. Two of the finest by Coysevox, called Peace and War, depicted scenes from the paintings of the Treaties of Aix-la-Chapelle and Nimégue in the *Galerie des Glaces*.

Because of his independent spirit, one of the sculptors, Pierre Puget, aroused the jealousy and enmity of his colleagues. He had made a model of a statue of Milon of Crotona, which the Marquis de Seignelay, Colbert's son, had seen at Marseilles, where Puget lived. The Marquis and Le Nôtre, who must have seen it too, liked it so much they insisted, despite Colbert's opposition, on having it brought to Versailles. When it arrived, it was received with hostility and was set up in an inconspicuous place until its merit was recognized by the King. Le Nôtre in contrast to other artists, treated Puget as a valued colleague; he presented him to the King, who bought two of his statues. But Mansart was opposed to Puget, so the disgruntled sculptor, considered by posterity one of the greatest in France, retired permanently to his home in the South.

It can readily be imagined how difficult it must have been to plant a vast park like Versailles within a few years. Le Nôtre had to procure fully grown trees wherever he could; it was impossible to wait for seedlings to grow. Elms and lindens were dug up from the forest of Compiègne, oaks and hornbeams from the woods of Flanders and Normandy, evergreen oaks from as far south as Dauphiné, and coniferous trees from the Vosges in the north. Madame de Sévigné told how, while out riding, she encountered strange convoys of "entire leafy forests being carried to Versailles," and said the trees "swayed like seesaws on ox-drawn wagons." Service trees (*Sorbus*) were planted in the *allées* because of their handsome foliage—as were also

Left: Painted lead figures, illustrating Aesop's Fables, in the maze at Versailles.
Right: Trellis in the same maze. Both engravings by Le Clerc.

107

elms and sycamores. Lindens were considered the best trees for shade in *allées*, as margins to tunnels of trelliswork, and for room-like gardens. To this day, in June and July the delicious fragrance of their blossoms is diffused throughout the park. The gardener Martin Trumel (who had worked at Vaux) collected them from the woods and planted them in a nursery, with other trees, on land beyond the *Petit Parc*.

In the shade, maples were planted, and, facing north, hazel bushes. Palisades were composed of white hawthorn although gardeners knew these shrubs were subject to disease. They were planted because, as André Mollet wrote, "Nightingales like them and therefore they are good for *bosquets*." Le Nôtre was careful to have each of the newly planted trees receive two barrels of water. Despite this attention, three-fourths of the trees transplanted from forests died.

Flowers were subsidiary in the scheme of a classical garden. There were a few places such as the *Parterre de Latone* and of the *Midi*, and at the Trianon, where there were masses of bedding-plants which produced subtle color effects.

To obtain flowers, Colbert often wrote to the admiral of the galleys to send plants to Paris from the south of France. In one letter he wrote, "You know it is necessary to have great quantities of flowers for the decorations of gardens of royal houses. Since there are many kinds in Provence, I beg you to purchase all the jonquils and tuberoses you can find and in general all the strange flowers which you think would contribute to the decoration and send them soon, so they can be planted next spring."

Millions of seeds of trees and shrubs were sown, cuttings set in sand, and scions grafted on stock by the hundreds of thousands. Flowers, too, were grown in fantastic numbers. To assure their survival after being transplanted, they were first shipped in pots from the nurseries to all the royal gardens; the King was never to see any immature or faded flowers but only plants at the height of their bloom. On one occasion at the Trianon, late in the reign, all the flowers were taken out and replaced between the time the King went indoors and the time he came out again a few hours later. To accomplish this uninterrupted floral display, over two million pots were in use at one time and these had to be carried forth and back continually, according to Le Nôtre.

Dr. Lister, an English visitor to France, wrote about the royal nursery in the Faubourg Saint-Honoré near the Tuileries, which was under the management of Monsieur Morly: "Here are several acres of young pines and cypresses . . . vast beds of stock July flowers (carnations), and all sorts of bulbs such as tulips, daffodils, crocuses and so forth. Eighteen million tulips and other bulbous flowers were sent to Marly alone, four times a year. From here he could plant and furnish in fourteen days any new garden the King could cause to be made." This was late in the century, but by 1667 the work was already well organized.

Bouquets brought in from the garden in June were composed of madonna lilies, poppies, lupines, anemones, carnations, peonies, and moss roses, all charmingly arranged for color and mass. Reproductions of such bouquets were woven into the chair coverings. Flowers were made into garlands and festoons, which were reproduced in wood, marble or bronze to decorate walls and furniture. They were painted on panels, and they framed the wall tapestries depicting Louis' victorious battles.

All the decorations at Versailles were carried out with grace, clarity, and, as time went on, with increasing delicacy, attributes which characterize French art and make it one of the great creative expressions of all time.

Despite the mythological symbols that clothed their ideas, Versailles, to the people who created it and lived there, was modern. The present-day observer, viewing the palace and park from a perspective of three hundred years, is keenly aware how every detail in the ensemble, from the great outdoor vistas and parterres to the tapestries, woodwork and even clocks on the mantels indoors, expresses the artistic spirit not only of the French people of that day but also of those who visit the park today—of their clarity, their sense of proportion and balance, and their love of subtle color.

CHAPTER IX

GREAT PROJECTS

1. CHANTILLY

ABOUT the same time that the park was begun at Versailles, Le Nôtre was called to Chantilly, and worked on it—while carrying out commissions elsewhere—for approximately twenty years. In one of two letters he wrote to the Earl of Portland two years before his death (in regard to work his nephew, Claude Desgots, was to carry out for the King of England), it can be seen he considered the park at Chantilly one of his masterpieces. "Remember," he wrote, "the gardens you have seen in France, Versailles, Fontainebleau, Vaux-le-Vicomte, the Tuileries and above all Chantilly." When he described it he was carried away by enthusiasm.*

Though a large portion of the work at Chantilly was destroyed during the French Revolution and the remaining parts are not fully restored, it is one of the finest parks in France because of the basic plan, the outstanding water parterre, the poetic treatment of woods, and the superb staircase.

The estate and castle at Chantilly is one of the most ancient in France, antedating the year one thousand. For centuries Kings had hunted wild boar there as guests of the de Condé family, which was a collateral branch of the Bourbons. During the minority of Louis XIII, Prince Henri II de Condé led a revolt against the throne and later became a partisan of

* See *A History of Gardening in England* by Evelyn Cecil. London, 1911, p. 192.

Richelieu. He was the father of Prince Louis II, known as the Grand Condé, who was the patron of Le Nôtre.

The Grand Condé was imperious and had a high temper. He never got over having been forced by his father, for political reasons, to marry Richelieu's niece Clair Clémence de Maillé-Brézé when he was deeply in love with Mademoiselle Marthe de Vigean. In his resentment he kept his wife in exile and later imprisoned her; yet he was a brilliant man and one of the ablest generals in Europe. At one time, when the spirit of revolt was strong in him, he had fought for Spain against his own country. Louis XIV forgave him for he felt it was wiser to be his friend than his enemy and treated him with so much understanding that Condé fought beside Turenne and won many battles for France.

Le Nôtre seems to have gotten on very well with the Grand Condé, difficult though the prince was. In the park there is a statue of Le Nôtre showing him seated and with plans in hand. The relationship between the artist, conscious of his gifts, and the great noble, is indicated in a passage (quoted by Corpechot) in Le Nôtre's letter of thanks when he had been granted a favor he requested for one of his nephews, the ten-year-old *Le Prince*, who was already a tonsured priest:

> *Monseigneur, not the honor which I had in embracing our Holy Father, the Pope, pleased me so much nor gave me so much joy as I experienced through the kindness you have shown in giving me the living which your Highness has refused to so many crowned heads, in order to gratify me with the present, for which I will be gratefully appreciative to you all my life. Monseigneur, the little prior will pray constantly for your prosperity and health and I shall continue to put my thought upon the embellishments of the parterres, fountains and cascades of your great garden at Chantilly. Being with respect, Monseigneur Your Highness, your most humble and obedient servant.*

For Le Nôtre, work at Chantilly must have offered a contrast to the work at Versailles. Here he had his nephew Claude Desgots and pupil Gittard assist him. There was none of the usual interference by Colbert with exhortations to keep down expenses nor, after the ministers death, by his

The great staircase leading up to the château at Chantilly. A fountain is in the foreground.
Engraving by Perelle.

successor Louvois plotting for personal power. Moreover, there was sufficient
water to carry out the grandiose plans. The Prince was a skilled engineer:
as a pastime he invented devices whereby pumps could bring water from
springs in the valley to a reservoir to be used for his cascades. Other advantages
were that the earth was fertile and the disposition of the land better adapted to
landscaping in the grand style.

At Chantilly the Prince entertained so many people there was
no room for their retainers in the palace, so inns had to be built to accommodate

them in the village. He surrounded himself with a coterie of writers who were attracted by his fine library and by the desire to meet each other. Among the writers who lived at Chantilly were Santeul the poet, and Jean de La Bruyère, who came originally to tutor the Prince's grandson but stayed on as one of the train. Boileau and La Fontaine were frequent visitors. At times Molière and his troupe would come to give his plays.

The superintendent was Vatel, who had held the same position under Fouquet. It was he who, when the King was being entertained and the fish did not arrive on time, committed suicide because he felt his honor was at stake. The King was so chagrined at this tragedy that he said thereafter he would not allow his hosts to provide food for him and his retinue.

The ancient château had been remodeled many times. It was shaped somewhat like a parallelogram and stood on low ground on an island in a long, narrow body of water. When Le Nôtre came upon the scene, about 1661, there was a terrace connected with the château by a bridge and functioning as a forecourt. From this terrace there was a view over the meadows below. To take full advantage of this view, Le Nôtre in a highly original and daring fashion used the terrace—instead of the house which was situated so much lower down—as his point of departure for the whole park. Because it was so important in the scheme of the park, the terrace was enlarged and embellished. An imposing ramp was built to lead up to it from the entrance driveway. At the top, where it dominated the whole scene, stood the statue of Condé's redoubtable Huguenot ancestor, the Connétable (High Constable) Anne de Montmorency. From the terrace, a stairway descends to the great water parterre below. Olympian in its proportions, it was called the *Grands Degrés.* At the time, it was considered one of Le Nôtre's outstanding accomplishments in architecture; by posterity, it is regarded, along with the stairways of the orangerie at Versailles, as among the very greatest triumphs of classic art. There is a boldness about a big stairway in a garden which, because of the sense of permanence it conveys, is far more satisfying than a sloping lawn. Stairways are exceedingly difficult to design successfully. They must be seen their whole length when viewed from above or below and must be in proportion to the whole garden. To be inviting to the visitor, and not to appear steep or wearisome to climb, the steps should be interrupted by platforms, like rests in music.

At one side of the *Grands Degrés* was the palace. Le Nôtre designed the statues which adorned the two wings on either side of the steps, for at Chantilly he seems to have taken over Le Brun's functions as designer. In a note to the Grand Condé (quoted by Lucien Corpechot), which evidently accompanied a drawing of the stairway, Le Nôtre says:

> *Here is all I can do to ornament the base of your great stairway. I hope it will please you as much as it does me. The river will be of stucco, the rest of the same. Bertier will place the vault, composed entirely of stone. The urn will spill as much water as you wish to give it; the feet of the figures the same; only three jets are required, as marked. This work can be done in a short time and with little expense: the sculptor is keen to do it and I assure Your Highness that I am with respect, Monseigneur, your very humble and obedient servant.*

In front of the stairway is a wide gravel-covered space broken in the center by a large circular basin. Beyond comes the great water parterre. On each side, as a frame, is an *allée* made of elms clipped *en table*, that is, rectangularly. One picture shows them to be tunnels but descriptions sound as if they were truly *allées* between tall trees as they are today. At the farther end, parallel to the terrace, is the canal. A wide arm coming from it at right angles, divides the parterre in two and forms a definite strong central axis. On either side of this arm of water is a water parterre. Each is composed of two identical designs consisting of four circular pools placed round a central, somewhat rectangular-shaped pool, with rounded baroque corners, all set in an ornamental carpet of plants.

The canal was the river Nonnette, an affluent of the Oise. Before work began at the park the stream had rippled gently through the meadows but Le Nôtre had it enter in "an astonishing fall" and continue through the gardens within stone banks for a mile and a half. It followed the bend in the valley, turned south within the park, and then flowed on in its original course.

Across the river, in a treatment similar to other hills in Le Nôtre's gardens, the green slope rose in grassy steps that carried the vista to the horizon. Like the other hills it was adorned with statues to provide scale and accents.

Chantilly. The water parterre and château. An engraving by Perelle.

Originally the basins in the water parterre foamed with fountains, around which were statues and vases filled with flowers, while the canal was gay with boats having brightly colored sails and pennants. Today, with less ornamentation, with the pools set quietly in grass, the basic horizontality, resulting from great expanses of water, is very marked and produces an extraordinary sense of serenity and dignity.

Chantilly. The water parterre today.

To the west of the parterre was a series of gardens called *La Canadière*, considered to be Le Nôtre's finest work at Chantilly; unfortunately it has been destroyed.

Every part of the estate, even to the chicken-yards and cow-stables, was adorned. The dairy was of white marble, its entrance decorated with paintings illustrating the *Fables* of La Fontaine. In the menagerie, a popular feature of princely gardens, there was a fountain of Narcissus and groups of painted lead figures similar to groups in the labyrinth at Versailles, again representing characters from the *Fables* of La Fontaine.

The French aristocrats were athletic and fond of sport: to amuse them there were a croquet-ground, a tennis court and targets for shooting the arquebus and crossbow.

Though today the forest at Chantilly is merely a remnant of what it was, it is still poetic and an example to anyone, anywhere, of how to plan and plant a wood in a park or garden. One entrance to the forest was and still is the dark opening out of green hedges abutting on the vaulted walk leading from the terrace. Within the forest, dimly lit roads, green with mossy surfaces, provide vistas through trees shorn of their lower branches and their trunks kept clear of underbrush. Other paths branch from these roads and lead to open places that are either circular or eight-sided, and at one time were bordered with clipped hornbeams. In Le Nôtre's time these openings were ornamented with vases or even surrounded with marble colonnades. From these openings, called *ronds points* or *pattes d'oie* (goose feet), the roads radiate starwise.

On days when hunts took place, the ladies in their carriages and the villagers on foot would wait there to see the sport. The pounding of horses' hooves would announce the approach of hunters. Suddenly a deer pursued by dogs and hunters would dash in a flash of color from the shaded woods out into sunlit openings and then dart back into the shadows. On other days the sun shining through the trees would light scenes similar to those painted by Watteau and Lancret—young men and women resting in a glade beside a statue, playing blindman's buff or eating picnic meals from silver dishes on a white cloth spread on the ground.

There were unexpected features in the forest, such as a chapel or hunting lodge. One of these surprises was the romantic house and garden of Sylvie built early in the century and altered by the Grand Condé. It could serve as a model for a small garden similarly situated today. Unfortunately, only the plans remain. The garden was rectangular in outline and had beds shaped somewhat triangularly. The whole was enclosed on three sides by graceful trellises pierced by gates, all in delicately patterned latticework. On the fourth side was the house. When this retreat was new, the Duchess of the period, Marie Orsini, had sheltered here the poet Théophile de Viau; later he was condemned by Parliament for his licentious poetry. In appreciation of her kindness he dedicated poems to her in which he referred to her as Sylvie; hence the name of the hidden house with its garden.

Louis XIV seems to have appreciated beautiful Chantilly. It is reported that on one of his visits there, he casually said to the Prince: "My cousin, you should give me Chantilly." The Prince replied diplomatically, "Chantilly is under your order; Your Majesty can regard me as your concierge."

II. SAINT-CLOUD

Another famous wooded park of Le Nôtre's was Saint-Cloud, situated on a high bank of the Seine on the road to Versailles. Roads recently put through the place have spoiled it to a considerable extent.

Though the gardens did not have the pomp of Versailles or the grandeur of Chantilly they were notable because of the brilliant handling of a hilly, uneven terrain and the way vistas were created in difficult and unfavorable circumstances. The place must have appeared more logical when the château, designed by the architects Le Pautre, Girard, and Mansart, was standing, because the park was centered on it.

Philippe d'Orléans, called *Monsieur*, only brother of Louis XIV, bought the estate in 1658. He was known for his fine taste and gaiety and also for his vicious habits. His first wife, whose influence was effective at Saint-Cloud, was his first cousin, the Princesse Henriette, sister of Charles II of England. She was unusually charming; when she died at twenty-eight, she was deeply mourned by the King and the court. Bossuet preached a moving sermon at her funeral. Her close friend, Madame de La Fayette, wrote about her with love and admiration.

Between the château and the river, not on axis with any part of the building, there were elaborate gardens, in which was the showy cascade designed by Bernini during his short and stormy visit to France a few years before.

True to his principles, Le Nôtre wished to create a feeling of space around the house. Though the hill rose sharply on the garden side, he managed to achieve a long vista from the front of the house and made the parterre look wider than it was by breaks in the banks on either side. A second vista led from a wing of the château where the ground sank and was more or less parallel to the river but some distance away from it. This vista began in an irregularly shaped pool and continued in a series of canals called *Les Goulottes*, very like the canals in twelfth century Moorish gardens at Granada. Beyond the canals, the vista continued to a semicircular, gravel-covered space, *La Lanterne*, and on through a triple *allée*. From *La Lanterne* walks radiated to meet *allées* from other circles. Five enormous *allées* radiated from one circle and six from

St. Cloud. An engraving of the gardens.

another to form star shapes throughout the woods, an extraordinary achievement on so uneven a piece of ground.

Besides roads through the woods, footpaths and a series of charming stairways led up the hill so gradually that they did not appear to be steep. While climbing them, the visitor was distracted from fatigue and exhilarated by a series of terraces so contrived that the one above was not seen until it was reached. The terraces were ornamented with pools, benches and statues. At each succeeding level the château below seemed to be growing smaller. From the summit one could see as far as Paris, with the pinnacles of *Nôtre-Dame* and the *Tour Saint-Jacques* gray under the blue and white skies.

On hot summer days it is still delightful to walk on the soft turf of the *allées* or climb from one terrace to the next, in that part of Saint-Cloud which is now a public park. When Dr. Lister visited Saint-Cloud in 1698, he wrote:

> *The gardens are vast in extent, twelve to fifteen miles in compass. Drove through the gardens with the physician of Madame in a coach, a privilege of that person . . . In the orangerie are trees in such huge cases that they need special machinery to move them; also oleanders, laurustinus; only ordinary and infructuous green on the walls here. In the garden are many arbors of trelliswork, pavilions and so forth of iron mixed with wood, painted green with honeysuckles running up them. These gardens have one hundred and fifty people always employed to keep them in order.*

III. SAINT-GERMAIN

Farther along the Seine, beyond Saint-Cloud and not far from Versailles, where the banks of the river are high and there is another distant view of Paris, is the castle of Saint-Germain, a favorite residence of French kings from the twelfth century. In Le Nôtre's day there were two castles, the ancient fortified building and the one called *Château Neuf*. The new château, built by Henry IV, was more like a barracks than a luxurious residence. When Louis XIII was a little boy he had played there with the children of Gabrielle d'Estrèes, his father Henry IV's mistress. The country was so wild that the gardens had to be fenced to protect the children from wolves, wild boars and brigands. Louis XIV was born here.

Other designers of royal gardens had worked there before Le Nôtre: Brauderie the elder and the Mollets. These designers laid out elaborate terraces built over a series of grottos decorated with paintings, shell work and mechanical contrivances for surprise-waters, a favorite form of practical joking of the period.

Improvements out-of-doors had been carried out during the ascendancy of Mademoiselle de La Vallière, Louis' favorite in his youth. She was romantic and liked to stroll in the moonlight. The château had been done over during the sway of Madame de Montespan, the favorite of Louis' middle years, who liked splendor and comfort.

When it was Le Nôtre's turn to take charge of the park at Saint-Germain, he confined himself to the parterre and he worked on it off and on from 1668 to 1673. Because there were two châteaux, it was difficult to place the parterre. Le Nôtre solved the problem by making two parterres, each oriented on the perpendicular axis of a château. However, one was on a slant. To fill the space between the two and act as a transition from slanting to straight lines, Le Nôtre made an irregularly shaped garden with three basins, each of a different shape. The parterre in front of the new château was so huge it could be viewed in its entirety only from the second-story windows. Because it was so big and bare of shade the people of Saint-Germain called it "Sénégal" in summer and "Siberia" in winter. In another part of the park Le Nôtre designed a *boulingrin* (an English type of parterre) in compliment to the English Princess Henriette.

The finest work Le Nôtre did at Saint-Germain was the *Grande Terrasse*. It was another of his great conquests over nature. The terrace consists of a splendid avenue extending for one and a half miles in a straight road parallel to the river Seine and high above it. The proportions are superb. A circle is at the near end of the great road and a hexagon at the far end. A walk for pedestrians and a road for carriages are separated by bands of turf. On one side are the great forest trees with their branches extending over the road; on the other is the river. A balustrade has been built here since Le Nôtre's day. The road was intended to connect the *Château Neuf* with the *Château du Val* located at the farther end of the park. Paths lead from it into the woods.

The forest was a hunting preserve, encircled by a wall. Deer were brought to it from the forest of Compiègne, and chestnuts were planted every year.

The alterations and upkeep of Saint-Germain were exceedingly expensive. The King lived there until he moved to Versailles, then seldom came back. However, the money was well spent for posterity: the terrace with its views of the river and of Paris provides one of the most beautiful walks in France and perhaps of its kind anywhere. Woods and terrace are the pride of the present citizens of Saint-Germain, who stroll through the parks, sit on the benches and picnic under the trees.

CHAPTER X

JOURNEYS TO ENGLAND AND ITALY

W HILE LE NÔTRE was finishing his work at Vaux and busily superintending alterations in the park at Fontainebleau, Charles II ascended the throne of England. Soon thereafter, Charles, through the French Ambassador, asked Louis to permit Le Nôtre to work for him. Louis wanted to be on good terms with the English, so he replied, "Although I always have need of Le Nôtre, who is very occupied with work for me at Fontainebleau, I shall willingly permit him to make the trip to England since the King desires it." Gabriel Mollet accompanied Le Nôtre* and stayed as the King's gardener.

Le Nôtre redesigned the parks at Whitehall and Greenwich; he laid out a semicircular garden at Hampton Court; he is credited with the gardens at Bush Hill Park between Edmonton and Enfield; and he made plans for the Duke of Devonshire at Chatsworth and for Lord Chesterfield at Bretby. Other gardens, among them Levens, have been attributed to him. Characteristically he introduced long, bold avenues and *pattes d'oie*, made terraces, and cut great vistas through the woods.

---

* The doubt sometimes expressed as to whether Le Nôtre actually went to England is groundless. Various documents and books, such as those by Cecil, Ward and Edward Walford, listed in my bibliography support all the statements made here. One document, for example, is a warrant issued on October 25, 1662, to permit "Le Nôtre, the King's architect, to transport six horses to France custom free as by royal warrant recited of the twenty-first of the same."

Le Nôtre found that the gardens in England followed earlier, much simpler models than those in France. The romantic, naturalistic garden, imitating nature, for which England has since become famous, did not develop until a hundred years later. Le Nôtre's work, with its unity and geometric patterns, had very little influence on the development of the English style. The English stressed individualism, not conformity. They were, moreover, so fond of their countryside that when they later created their own style they reproduced their natural woods and meadows.

Nor does Le Nôtre seem to have gained much from his visit to England. He was there too short a time and was too busy to do more than carry out his commissions. He had so much to do in France that he hurried back, leaving the work in England to be supervised by his assistants, with French gardeners to take care of the gardens after they were finished.

Much later, William III sent the Duke of Portland to France in 1698 with a splendid retinue to try—it was in vain—to dissuade Louis from granting the exiled James II a home. Evidently at that time the Duke commissioned Le Nôtre to make plans for a royal garden, probably Kensington. However, Le Nôtre was too old to travel abroad and instead sent his nephew, Claude Desgots, to superintend the gardens.

The visit to England had been at royal command and during his busiest years. But when he was sixty-six years old, after he had accomplished his important work, Le Nôtre went to Italy on a pleasure journey. In contrast to other travelers, who came to study ancient and Renaissance art, he went as a triumphant artist. Correspondence in regard to the visit shows that he was considered the greatest living architect of gardens and a source of intense national pride. The French obviously thought he was a man from whom the Italians, who had once taught them, could now learn.

Undoubtedly Le Nôtre had long wanted to see Italian landscape art in its native setting; he had been urged to come by Charles Errard, head of the French Academy in Rome, but had not been able to leave France because of the pressure of work. When he was ready to go, he needed an excuse, and this he found in the objective of looking after Claude Desgots, his nephew (later his assistant), who was a student-pensioner at the French Academy in Rome.

When Colbert heard of the projected trip, he asked Le Nôtre to make a report on the work of the Academy. He also asked him to try to settle the matter of a statue that Bernini had been asked to make of the King. There had been much controversy about this work, with the French artists opposing the Italians and insisting that such an important statue be made by a Frenchman. By requesting him to handle this difficult situation, Colbert showed how much confidence he had in Le Nôtre's tact and judgment. "Le Nôtre is going to Rome," he wrote to Charles Errard; "you will not fail to give him all the assistance you can and to tell him everything that is going on in the Academy and how you plan to instruct the young men I send you. You know his ability and you should make it a point to follow any advice he may give you about the studies of students as about everything in regard to the said Academy."

The same day Colbert wrote to the Duc d'Estrées, French Ambassador to Italy, in whose home Le Nôtre was to live during his visit: "The Sieur Le Nôtre, whom you know, is going to Italy not so much from curiosity as to look carefully for something beautiful enough to merit being copied in the royal dwellings or to furnish him with new ideas for the beautiful gardens he creates every day for the satisfaction and pleasure of His Majesty. In short I am telling you enough so that you will give him all the assistance which he will require in order to have the *entrée* to all the palaces and fine houses in the neighborhood of Rome."

Le Nôtre traveled to Italy in excellent company, for he went with the Duchesse de Sforza, mother of Madame de Montespan, and her sister and brother-in-law, the Duc and Duchesse de Nevers. The two duchesses belonged to a family noted for its wit and beauty. The Maréchal de Vivonne was also of the party.

For years Le Nôtre had studied and known about Italian art from paintings and prints and from descriptions of returned travelers. When he came face to face with the intricate, terraced gardens he said—even though they were entirely different from his own grandiose parks—that he was "surprised to find only what he had pictured." Apparently he was not so enthusiastic about them as he had expected to be. He told Desgots, who was his constant companion and interpreter during the stay in Rome, "The Italians have no taste in gardens which can approach ours. They do not know how to make them." Similarly, when Bernini had been in France he had said the French liked only "feminine" art. When asked his opinion of the gardens at Saint-Cloud, the master of baroque art had said that they were too perfect, that "one should dissemble artifice and try to give objects a more natural appearance, but in France in general the contrary was done." It is almost unnecessary to add that the remarks of both artists were colored by national pride.

The story of the visit of Le Nôtre to the Pope is widely known and told in France. Almost immediately after his arrival, the Pope asked to see him. The Pope was Innocent XI, with whom Louis had disputed about the rights of his ambassadors and the privilege of appointing French bishops. The garden architect went to the audience accompanied by Desgots, carrying with him drawings of the park and fountains at Versailles. The visit was described in a letter Desgots wrote to Bontemps, first *valet de chambre* at Versailles.

Bontemps read it to the King when the latter asked how Le Nôtre was getting on in Italy. According to the letter, after Le Nôtre had made his reverence to the Pope, His Holiness asked to see the plans of Versailles about which he had heard so much, and Le Nôtre unrolled his drawings. The Pope was impressed at the number of canals, fountains, jets and cascades. He remarked that it must take at least a river to furnish such a prodigious amount of water. Le Nôtre replied that there was no river, but that the water had been collected in ponds and carried by tiled conduits to large reservoirs. The Pope was astonished, and asked whether this had not cost enormous sums.

"Holy Father, it has not exceeded two hundred millions as yet," bragged Le Nôtre.

At this the Pope's amazement rose "to such a degree it would be difficult to describe." Delighted at the effect he was having, Le Nôtre exclaimed: "Now I have no regret in dying. I've seen the two greatest men in the world, Your Holiness and the King, my master."

"There is a big difference," replied the Pope. "The King is a great and victorious prince while I am a poor priest and the servant of the servants of God. He is young and I am old."

This so charmed Le Nôtre that he tapped the Pope on the shoulder and said, "Reverend Father, you are in good health and you will bury the whole Sacred College."

His Holiness, who understood French, laughed at this, and Le Nôtre, carried away by the Pope's friendliness, threw his arms around him and kissed him.

When Bontemps reached this point in the letter, the King laughed and the Duc de Crequy, first gentleman of the bedchamber, said he would wager a thousand *louis d'or* that it did not go as far as a kiss.

"Do not bet that," observed Louis. "When I return from a campaign, Le Nôtre kisses me and he could well have kissed the Pope."

Evidently the pleasure of the meeting between the Pope and Le Nôtre was mutual. The Pope asked to see Le Nôtre again and requested him to redo the Vatican gardens in the French style. It has been said Le Nôtre made plans for the gardens at the Villa Pamphili and at the Villa Ludovisi and many others. However, these designs had little effect on the gardens of Italy, which grew out of the life of the people and their land, and were already fully developed before Le Nôtre came.

Le Nôtre also attended to the matter of the Bernini statue. He had it sent to France but because of the controversy it was given an inconspicuous place behind the *Lac des Suisses* at Versailles.

In a letter—which is now missing—Le Nôtre gave Colbert his impressions of the French Academy in Rome. Colbert answered, "You are right in saying that genius and good taste come from God and that it is very difficult to give it to men." Then the Minister added, "Even if these academies do not develop great artists, they serve to perfect the workmen and give us the best France has ever had . . . Come back as soon as you can."

CHAPTER XI

OLD GARDENS REMODELED

THE ROYAL PARKS WERE also to be remodeled by Le Nôtre. Alterations carried out during his years as superintendent of buildings bear his unmistakable signature. It must have been a special pleasure for him to make changes in the Tuileries, where he had practically grown up; his family had worked in the gardens for three generations, and he lived in a house in the gardens from his middle years until his death. Undoubtedly after a trip to Versailles or some more distant place, he would stroll along the paths of the Tuileries gardens in the evening to supervise the planting and cultivating. He had probably thought out exactly how he would change the place long before he was called to the task.

At that time the grounds of the Tuileries adjoined the walls of Paris. The château had been designed by Philibert de Lorme for Catherine de Medicis in 1564. (The name Tuileries came from pottery works previously on the property.) Because almost every king wanted his parks and palaces to suit his special tastes and interests, the gardens were altered many times. Jean Le Nôtre, André's father, had worked here with Pierre Neveu in 1609 under the supervision of Claude Mollet. Oliver de Serres had a hand in designing the gardens, and after him Jacques Boyceau, contemporary of Jean Le Nôtre, had been designer and head gardener for many years. During the reign of Henry IV, the terraces between the castle and the old moat that separated

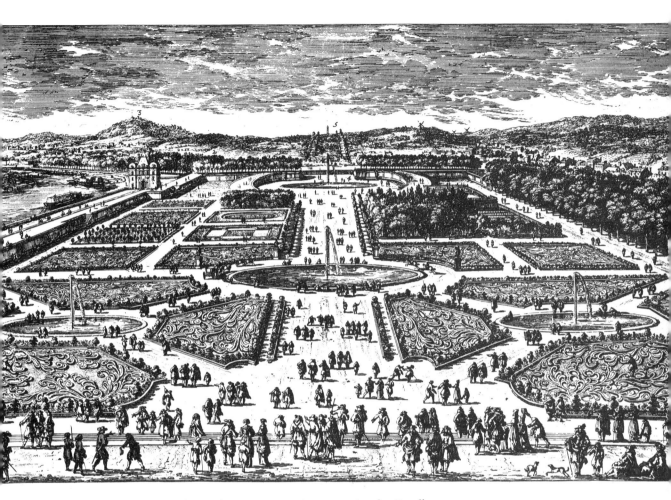

The Tuileries in 1680. An engraving by Perelle.

the Tuileries from the Louvre were extended and the beds in them were executed in intricate designs by Claude Mollet. He was also in charge of twenty thousand white mulberry trees that were planted along the *allées* on the north side in what appears to have been an unsuccessful attempt to grow silk worms in northern France.

Le Nôtre remodeled the park so attractively that a good part of it has remained practically unchanged, through revolutions, wars and invasions, to the present day. When times were prosperous, the beds and borders here, as in other former royal gardens now belonging to the state, were

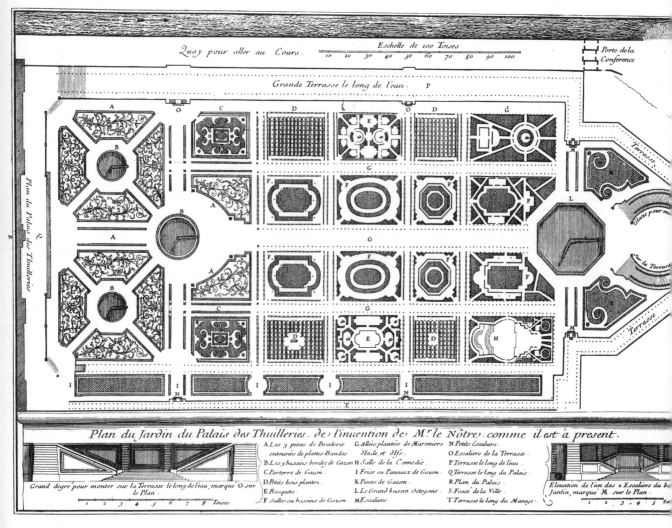

The Tuileries. Plan of the gardens by Le Nôtre.

planted with flowers and kept in exquisite order. When times were hard, as before the Revolution, or right after the Franco-Prussian war, when trees were cut down for kindling wood, or right after the First World War, the gardens were neglected and shabby. One great change occurred after 1871 when the palace was burned to the ground and the site was covered with gardens to join those in front of the Louvre.

The central vista of this park has become a broad avenue in a great city; today it begins in a crowded square in front of a wing of the old Louvre. In Le Nôtre's time it began in a great open space in front of the Tuileries. From there it led through the center of the garden over the great octagonal pool. It went out through a gateway pierced in the old ramparts, crossed the Cours-la-Reine, part of which was later to become the Place de la Concorde, and led on in a tremendously broad roadway lined with trees (the present avenue des Champs Élysées), up to a distant hill, marked by an obelisk where the Arc de Triomphe now stands. Thence it continued, in much more modest proportions, as a road all the way to Versailles.

Here was the first avenue in Europe to cut through the clutter of buildings and narrow walks that cramped every medieval city and lead out into the open countryside. This clearing away of medieval debris and widening of horizons in both cities and gardens was in a way an expression of the same spirit that inspired explorations to distant lands as well as scientific advances. Moreover, providing for greater and faster-moving traffic by means of a wide avenue, Le Nôtre facilitated communication between Paris and the châteaux of Versailles and Saint-Germain.

The idea of a straight avenue extending through a city was an adaptation of Le Nôtre's great park and garden vistas. It was copied far and wide. At Williamsburg in colonial Virginia, a long straight avenue leads from the college to the House of Burgesses. Later in Washington, capital of a new country, Pennsylvania Avenue was laid out in a straight line from the White House to the buildings that house Congress.

Le Blond, always carping, wrote of the main vista that it was not open enough; he said, "You can scarce see the door of the Great Pavilion from the end of it." He thought this effect resulted from the fact that the chestnuts along the sides were planted too closely. The truth was that the whole treatment was regal in character, from the parterres which provided a majestic setting for the château and the placing of each feature with a broad space round it, to the paths so wide and convenient as still to be perfectly suited to the crowds who use this park today.

In the quieter parts of the park nowadays, people sit on the benches, read their papers, make love, and watch children playing ball down *allées* where memories of kings of France still linger. Here when Le Nôtre was a little boy, Louis XIII rode out to hunt with a falcon on his wrist and accompanied by his favorite, Albert de Luynes. One day according to an oft-told tale, the King chased a bear into the gardens, and saw it rout the

131

gardeners and finally in desperation throw itself into a pool near the orangerie. On sunny afternoons Le Nôtre undoubtedly saw the blond and beautiful Anne of Austria, mother of Louis XIV, come into the garden with her ladies-in-waiting, overheard them tease her about the handsome English Duke of Buckingham, and then saw them pick up their heavy trains and play tag down the *allées* between the statues and around the pools.

Before Le Nôtre began his alterations, the gardens had been crowded with activities similar to those of precincts within a medieval fortress. They were so noisy with the hammering of blacksmiths, rumble of heavy wagons, and the tramping of soldiers that the songs of birds were drowned out and the splashing of water in the fountains could be heard only close by.

His first task was to clear the garden of its clutter. He began with the bank along the Seine. Because the land sloped considerably from the Seine on one side to the rue Saint-Honoré and the Couvent de Feuillants on the other, Le Nôtre made an absolutely level space in the center, and then on either side built a terrace planted with trees to form a frame. These terraces with their walks are still in existence. Under the trees on each terrace were shaded walks; on the street side of these one could look down on people walking among the flower beds or on the river side, watch the barges moving along the Seine, grimy ones laden with barrels and bales, and others, elaborately carved and gilded, carrying royal or noble travelers. These terraces turned at a right angle near the octagonal pool at the end of the garden and then, facing the château curved in graceful ramps while sloping down to the lower level.

This lower level between the terraces Le Nôtre treated in the old checkerboard pattern, a design well suited to a garden so rich in memories. But he gave a new touch to it; the space was divided into four blocks of four each, eight on either side of the wide central vista. As shown on an old plan they were not all the same size, for the four in the third row were much smaller than the others while those in the fourth row were much the longest. Undoubtedly this was intended to counteract the effects of perspective and make them all appear alike when viewed from the parterre in front of the palace. Each division was treated as a separate unit. In some of the plots there were *boulingrins*, that is, grassy plots traversed by sanded lines to form a pattern and enclosed with closely trimmed trees, often with pleached branches. In other units, groves of trees were planted *quincunx*, a pattern descended from Roman days, that is the lines are parallel, equidistant and form parallelograms.

Dr. Lister, who visited the Tuileries in 1698, reported:

One of its features was an amphitheatre with a stage, pit and settings leading on to the stage, very pretty from all sides, close allées leading into it. Nothing can be more pleasant than that garden where, in the groves of trees, at the latter end of March, the blackbirds and throstles and nightingales sing sweetly all morning, and that, as it were, within the city, for no fowling is suffered here near this city and the fields around the town are everywhere full of partridges and hares and other game. The middle walk between eight and nine at night in June is the most agreeable place in the world at that hour and time of year. However, when it rains in the Tuileries, the gardens are shut up and one walks in the dirt some days afterwards.

The third largest garden in Paris after the Tuileries and Luxembourg was that of Cardinal Richelieu, now close to the Théâtre Français. During his lifetime it was called the *Palais-Cardinal* and after it became the property of the crown, the *Palais-Royal*. Today shops surround the park on three sides and a government office is on the fourth. When the Cardinal owned the place he did not permit his tenants to have windows facing his gardens for like all persons with dictatorial power he lived in constant fear; when the park became royal property this was changed.

John Evelyn, visiting the gardens in 1662, wrote they were too narrow for the palace; he speaks of "sweet rows of limes, a canal for water" and "the rich and noble fountain in the garden" but he also says there was not much water in it. Ten years later the gardens saw extensive changes; captions under contemporary prints credit Le Nôtre with being their author.

Again he used the plan of an old-time garden. In front of the palace he made a parterre flanked by a double row of elms divided in the center by a long axial *allée* interrupted at intervals, as were those at Meaux and Widcville, by two round basins with jets of water. White statues rose from box-bordered beds, gleaming against the green of trees behind them. A *berceau de treillage* (tunnel of latticework), similar to the one at Blois, was made for the garden.

Reports tell us how thoroughly Le Nôtre prepared the ground here. He had four feet of top soil and much fertilizer carried into the garden

The Tuileries. Bosquet.

for the trees and flowers. After the plants had been set, he had the whole place watered every day for three weeks. Dr. Lister, who came to the garden twenty years later, said it was not very well kept, "nor hath it anything elegant in it but the good order and disposition of its shady walks and parterres." Today the tree-shaded walks are still much frequented by Parisians.

French royalty had always been fond of Fontainebleau, at that time a two-days' journey from Paris. Each ruler in turn added features to the castle or park. Francis I, who established an Italian colony there in 1527, had elaborate gardens laid out, including a *grand parterre*, a *Jardin de Diane*, fish ponds, canals and pools, and a grotto. Later, Henry IV spent enormous sums on the palace grounds. He built cascades on axis with the *grand parterre* and connected by a canal.

Queen Anne, who was especially fond of Fontainebleau, spent the summer of 1646 there. It was so hot that the young King, along with his mother and the ladies and gentlemen of the court, went swimming in the river beyond the forest. According to Madame de Motteville, "The Queen and all who accompanied her wore grey linen chemises which reached to the ground; even the King and his governor wore the same." When the King was a gay young man, there was another summer at Fontainebleau. After bathing in the river, the young people would ride back to the château through the woods in the evening, "a thousand plumes on their heads."

Le Nôtre realized that the existing gardens were in harmony with the rambling old house and in the same style; he advised the King to leave the place much as his ancestors had handed it on to him. However, Louis could not resist doing something to Fontainebleau. So Le Nôtre enlarged the *grand parterre* and the canal. To keep the parterre in the same period as the building, he left it flat, with the result that it appears to be enormous. He also rearranged the beds and reshaped the lake, making the lines more regular. The bosquets north and south of the canal, and the *rond point* with its radiating avenues leading through the woods, are also obviously the work of Le Nôtre.

When Evelyn came to Fontainebleau he noted in his diary: "The park about the palace is very large, the grand canal an English mile in length, at the end of which rise three jetties in the form of *fleur-de-lis* of great height; about the margin are excellent walks planted with trees. The carp come familiarly to hand to be fed." The carp do the same to this day, but today much of the garden is gone, swallowed up by the town.

Besides remodeling old gardens belonging to royalty, Le Nôtre modernized a great many famous gardens belonging to the nobility. The French have loved their old places so much that they have maintained them through the centuries as a precious heritage from a rich past. This often necessitated many personal adjustments and sacrifices.

135

Twenty-two miles south of Paris is Courances, an exquisite old house and garden. It has been restored by Duchêne and is beautifully kept by the present owners, who have also introduced a modern flower garden at one side well hidden by shrubbery. An old French jingle says,

"Les Bois de Fleury
Les Parterres de Cely
Les Eaux de Courances
Sont trois merveilles en France."

and truly the waters at Courances murmur like a song.

The Estate was old in Le Nôtre's day for it originated in the thirteenth century. The château then standing had been built at the time of Henry II, in the sixteenth century. The main entrance stairway with its baroque twists and flourishes is similar to the one at the nearby château of Fontainebleau and was made by the same builder. The main house, three little gatehouses, and a parterre, are on an island separated from the rest of the park by the wide, still surface of an ancient moat. The buildings, of red brick, with gray stone coigns, are crowned by steep roofs covered with blue slate.

When Claude Galland, a prominent member of parliament, owned Courances, Henry IV and Louis XIII were entertained there; so was Richelieu, who rode over from his nearby château of Fleury. Galland made changes in the place; as did his son, and it must have been during the time when the latter lived there that Le Nôtre was called in to lay out the park.

The main motif in the gardens, the sound of tumbling waters, is first heard at the entrance driveway, for there it gushes from the mouths of dolphins into two long canals in front of plane trees bordering the roadway.

The gardens, typical of all classical examples, are centered on the house and form a unit with it. They begin at the terrace, which is divided in three parts to correspond to the three gatehouses at the entrance. The main axis, similar to many in Le Nôtre's parks, leads across the parterre, over a series of pools and grass plots all framed by woods, and terminates in a statue on a slight elevation and against a background of trees. The distinguishing quality is peacefulness, arising from the harmony of proportions, the masterly grading, the dominance of quiet blue and green colors, the almost imperceptible changes in levels, and, over all, the lulling sound of the waters.

The Tuileries. Looking toward the Arc de Triomphe.

Through the woods, made interesting by ponds and avenues, comes a surprise; it is a secondary axis similar to the one at Sceaux and probably of the same period. Here, however, it does not consist of elaborate waterfalls but of a long silent canal stepped on different levels; this is actually the River Ecolle made to flow between parallel banks.

Le Nôtre must have enjoyed designing the ornamentation, for there is something so gay and so right about them. The pedestals, instead

Rambouillet. Parterre.

138

Courances. The gardens as seen from the château.

of being of white marble, are of brick with stone coigns to harmonize with the house; and the corners of the pools are stepped.

About thirty miles from Paris is Rambouillet, now the country house of French presidents. The Duc de Montausier bought it in 1669 and called in Le Nôtre to plan the park. There was abundant water on the place and Le Nôtre made original use of it. The castle was old and asymmetrical, a picturesque building with pointed turrets. The whole building seemed to face in one direction. So Le Nôtre with his unfailing sense for the right solution focused the principal axis from a wing. In front of this wing he made a terrace, across the foot of which he had a fine balustrade built. Then came a unique scheme of waters not duplicated anywhere else. From a narrow channel below the parterre and parallel to it he spread out three canals fanwise, all terminating in a second canal parallel to the first. The central canal, the widest, carried the main axis which was prolonged beyond the water by a greensward that rose slightly and was framed by woods.

Not far from Rambouillet was Maintenon, which had been bought by the former Madame Scarron; when the King raised the estate to a marquisate, he called the lady who was to be his wife Madame de Maintenon. Ninon de Lenclos, who was not received at court but whose witty sayings were quoted and relished there, said, "*En ce cas c'est Madame Maintenant.*"

"Le Nôtre, famous architect," wrote Mademoiselle d'Aumale, companion to Madame de Maintenon, was sent by the King "to adjust this beautiful piece of land" and "help her in her plans for making the château comfortable."

Madame de Maintenon was a brunette, had a beautiful figure, and her conversation was called "delicious." She had come to court originally as the governess of the children of the King and Madame de Montespan and had advanced herself in the King's eyes partly by the striking contrast she offered to Madame de Montespan and partly by stressing piety and goodness. She came into favor with the passing of the King's youth, at a time of military reverses abroad and difficulties at home, when, to meet expenses, the King's silver, which had been made at the Gobelins and was the pride of Le Brun, had to be melted down.

Rambouillet. Showing the quincunx layout of trees.

She was bigoted and frugal; avoided spending much money at Maintenon and thus a minimum of work was done on the château. During her first five years there, the park developed slowly. Le Nôtre widened the moat through which the river Eure flowed, giving the banks graceful lines and broken curves. As at Courances, he had the moat encircle both the house and the little parterre at the foot of the château. The parterre was symmetrical; its center was rounded into a peninsular-like projection that extended into the river, flowing out of the moat and continuing in a straight line at right angles to the château. Some distance from the château the river was crossed by the high arches of the aqueduct that was intended to carry the waters from the Eure to Versailles but was never finished.

Thus Le Nôtre used the old moat, the new bed of the river and the aqueduct to make a picture very like those painted by Claude Lorraine or, a century later, by Hubert Robert from ruins contrived for effect in romantic gardens. The view could be enjoyed from the terrace on sunny days and from the windows of the old château when the vista was softened by the blue-gray of mist or rain.

Madame de Maintenon seldom came there; eventually she gave the place to her niece, the Duchesse de Noailles, whose descendants have kept it to the present day, much as it was. It, too, is now open to the public.

On the Seine between Versailles and the Faubourg-Saint-Germain, in Paris, was Meudon, an estate famous in the sixteenth century. Its château and park no longer exist. The house had been designed by the architect Philibert de Lorme for Cardinal Charles of Lorraine, uncle of Mary, later Queen of Scotland; the Cardinal had also been Minister of State to Henry II and leader of the Catholic faction opposing the Huguenots. Abel Servien, who was associate superintendent of finance with Fouquet, bought Meudon from the Guise family and carried out extensive alterations contemporaneously with those at Vaux-le-Vicomte. Le Vau was his architect but it is not known who designed the park. Thirty years later, in 1683, Meudon was bought by Michel Le Tellier, marquis de Louvois, Colbert's rival, who employed Le Nôtre to re-do his park.

The plan lacked the usual clarity and precision of Le Nôtre's work, perhaps because Louvois insisted on his own ideas. Critics of the gardens thought they were too up-and-down-hill for comfortable walking. Le Blond

Rambouillet. An engraving by Rigaud of the treatment of the original canal.

wrote that whereas at Chantilly, Sceaux, and Saint-Cloud, the terrace walks and waters fitted into the picture and the statuary heightened the effects, at Meudon, they appeared cluttered and crowded. He thought Meudon "very strange and Sceaux, Saint-Cloud, and Chantilly very natural."

However, Louis liked the place, perhaps because, as Perelle had written under his drawing of the park, "Meudon has one of the finest views in the world." After the death of Louvois, the King exchanged it for Choisy with the widow, who said, diplomatically, that she was well pleased to have a smaller home. In his *Memoires* Dangeau, the King's valet, described the King's visit to Meudon on June 5, 1695: "The day before yesterday the King was at Meudon. Monsieur Le Nôtre showed him the beauties of the house and gardens and upon leaving them said, in this chaffing manner, 'Sire, I am delighted you have Meudon; but I would have been sorry if you had had it sooner for you would not have made it so beautiful.'" This refers to the great sums of money spent there by Louvois. The King gave the place

143

to his son, the Dauphin, who, according to a caption on a contemporary print, "made of it the finest house in the universe."

Gay, vivid Marguerite de Valois, first wife of Henry IV, owned Issy and captured the stream behind her château to play the fountains in her garden. In Le Nôtre's time the place belonged to the Princesse de Conti. Le Blond commented on the place, "Although the grounds were irregular and steep, this clever man (Le Nôtre) has made a *chef-d'oeuvre*." The gardens were long and narrow and all on one side of the house.

The fountains at Issy are mentioned in a poem, *La petite olympe d'issy*:

> *"Mainte belle scource endoyante*
> *De coulant de cent lieux divers*
> *Maintieunent terre verdoyante*
> *Et ses arbrisseaux toujours verts."*

In the sixteenth century the poet Ronsard mentions the gardens at Conflans. They were close to Paris and situated at the juncture of the Seine and Marne. In 1673 François Harlay de Champvallon, Archbishop of Paris, bought the place. He was an urbane churchman, only mildly opposed to the Port Royalists, a devout group of Puritancal Catholics, and was famous for his sermons at Nôtre Dame. It was he who arranged Madame de Montespan's divorce and, after the change of favorites, married the King to Madame de Maintenon. Like almost every other man of note in France he called in Le Nôtre "to correct the faults of the land." After Le Nôtre had finished changing the place, it must have been utterly charming. He made three terraces stepping down to the river. To one side there was a wide tunnel of latticework that led to a highly ornate and elegant pavilion on the bank of the river. Its ceiling, painted by Lesueur, had a frieze of shells representing the play of tritons and dolphins.

Saint-Simon gives an amusing description of the Archbishop strolling in the gardens "with his dear friend the Duchesse de Lesdiguières whom he saw every day in his life, either at her own house or at Conflans where he had laid out a delicious garden that was kept so strictly clean that as the two walked, gardeners followed at a distance and effaced their footsteps with rakes."

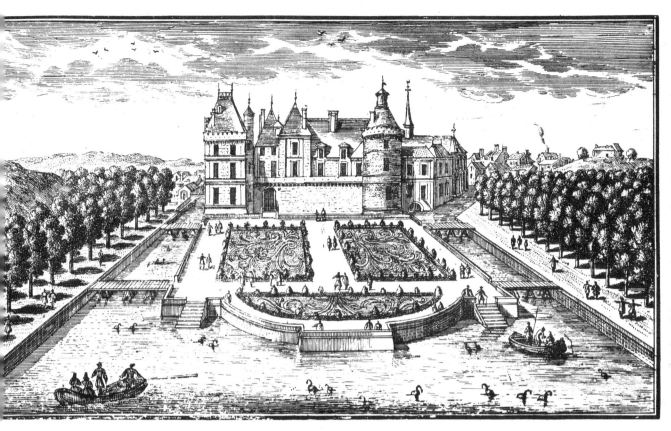

Château de Maintenon. An engraving showing the treatment of the moat.

The park at les Rochers in Brittany was famous because it belonged to Madame de Sévigné, who spent much time there and called in Le Nôtre to redesign it. This witty, brilliant woman, as famous for her charm as for her matchless letters, says little about her gardens. She mentions them only in passing: "As to my labyrinth, it is born, it has a greensward, and the palisades are elbow high. It is a pleasant spot." In May 1671, she writes: "Well, my daughter, here I am in this dear Rochers. Can one revisit these *allées*, these mottos (she hung quotations on her trees) this little cabinet, these books, this room without expiring of sadness?"

In the same summer she writes, "We went for a walk and sat down in the depths of the woods"; while the others played tennis, she sat

Maintenon. View of the unfinished aqueduct.

and gossiped with her friend Madame de Chaulnes. Four years later she wrote, "I have found the woods of an extraordinary beauty and sadness, alas! The trees you saw so small have now grown to be tall and straight and of a perfect beauty; they are pruned and form a pleasant shade; they are forty or fifty feet high. Here is a little breath of maternal love. Just think, I planted them all and I saw them, as Monsieur de Montbazon said of his children, 'No bigger than that.'"

CHAPTER XII

GARDENS FOR THE GENTRY

D URING his long life—eighty-one years—Le Nôtre must have designed about a hundred gardens. Almost everyone in France— and some foreigners as well—who wanted a garden came to him for a plan. It is astonishing what fertility of imagination he displayed and what a high standard he maintained. For each client he devised some original feature; each great park or small garden reflected the character of its owner; each was well suited to the location and to the house upon it.

Some of his most charming gardens were designed for the nobility and the gentry. One of these was Clagny, three miles beyond Versailles. It was designed, laid out and planted, and then disappeared so quickly that it seemed like a wish momentarily fulfilled by rubbing an Aladdin's lamp; for it was begun in 1674, abandoned eleven or so years later, and de- molished shortly thereafter.

Originally the place was built to provide a home for "*Mes- seigneurs les enfants naturels de Roi.*" Their mother, Madame de Montespan, took an active interest in the planning and execution and looked upon Clagny as belonging to her. She was Françoise-Athenais de Pardaillan de Rochechouart and had been married to a great noble, the Marquis de Montespan, who went into mourning when she became the King's mistress. The Marquise was a radiant blond, the most beautiful woman in France, a brilliant conversationalist, exceedingly witty and entertaining but with a sharp tongue. She had the bearing of a queen but was temperamental and fond of gambling for high stakes. Louis was fascinated and enthralled by her and she bore him seven children. It was during her ascendancy, which occurred between the treaties of Aix-la-Chapelle in 1668 and Nimégue (ten years later), that extravagance was wildest and ornament richest at court. On the other side of the medal, and to her credit, it was she who encouraged writers and artists and was the leader, during her sway, of the exquisitely civilized atmosphere that pervaded the social life of the court.

However, when her influence began to wane, Madame de Montespan hesitated to stay at Clagny and be away from Versailles where Madame de Maintenon kept telling the King he ought to renounce her because, both being married, their relationship was a double adultery. At last there was a reluctant move to Clagny on the part of "*la Belle*," as Madame de Montespan was called. There Bossuet, the King's spiritual advisor, came to see her daily to exhort her to lead a better life. He always brought a letter from the King which he mistakenly thought was in the same tenor as his talks. However, in the course of time the lady returned to Versailles. She was so ambitious and at the same time so unsure of her position that she consulted la Voisin, a woman of criminal habits, to obtain charms and aphrodisiacs with which to dose the King so as to hold his affections. Finally, when la Voisin was involved in a notorious poison case and Madame de Montespan's dealings with her were exposed, her hold on the King was weakened, though she remained at Court several years longer.

In keeping with Madame de Montespan's extravagance, the house at Clagny cost more than two million *livres*. Like the costly jewels and clothes she wore at fêtes, the place expressed her personality in the originality of its details and the fine taste with which they were executed. Le Pautre was to have been the architect and was disappointed when Le Nôtre secured the work for twenty-eight-year-old Jules Hardouin-Mansart. Another protégé, his nephew Le Bouteux, worked in the gardens as his uncle's assistant.

The gardens were much admired. Perhaps some of their appeal was due to their being a smaller and more intimate version of a style familiar on a much larger scale.

Madame de Sévigné came to Clagny for the first time in July, 1675, before the garden was finished, and found twelve hundred men still at work. The following month she came again and wrote:

We were at Clagny—what can I tell you about it? It is the palace of Armide. The building is all finished; the gardens are completed, you know the ability of Le Nôtre. He left a little dark wood standing, which is most effective. There is a grove of orange trees in huge tubs and one can walk among them and they are so high that the allées between them are shaded. To hide the tubs there are hedges on both sides, waist high, all in flower with tuberoses, roses, jasmine, and carnations. It is assuredly the most beautiful, the most astonishing and most enchanting novelty one can possibly imagine; this wood is much admired.

The idea of growing flowers among hedges was popular in Italy and had been described in one of Boccaccio's stories. The effect was contrived by placing pots filled with carnations and other flowers among the branches of the hedge plants.

Nicodème Tessin, who came there after Madame de Montespan's disgrace, wrote: "At Clagny the château is not furnished and the garden not well kept; the two *bosquets* (gardens within a garden) are very pretty; the one on the right which I sketched is made of thorny hawthorn; it is 250 ells long and 180 wide (roughly 937 feet by 675); the *bosquet* on the left is the same size but even prettier. It is planted in *charmille* (hornbeam) with chestnuts at the corners."

In addition to the features described by the visitors just quoted there were summer houses of trelliswork, constructed by Dutch craftsmen who were imported because they excelled in this kind of work. The houses were painted *vert de montagne* and had Ionic columns. There was a little menagerie in the garden and of course there were fountains. An original touch was a cover of tiles for the boundary walls. A rustic note was provided by beehives and by planting thyme and sage for the bees.

Though the garden has disappeared, the plans and drawings still exist. If they were somewhat simplified to suit our time they could still be applied to a park or private garden.

Historians and diarists of the period often mention *La Grande Mademoiselle*, the tall, blond Duchesse de Montpensier, who was daughter of Gaston d'Orléans, brother of Louis XIII, and consequently a first cousin of Louis XIV. She was imperious and silly, a woman of fashion who imagined

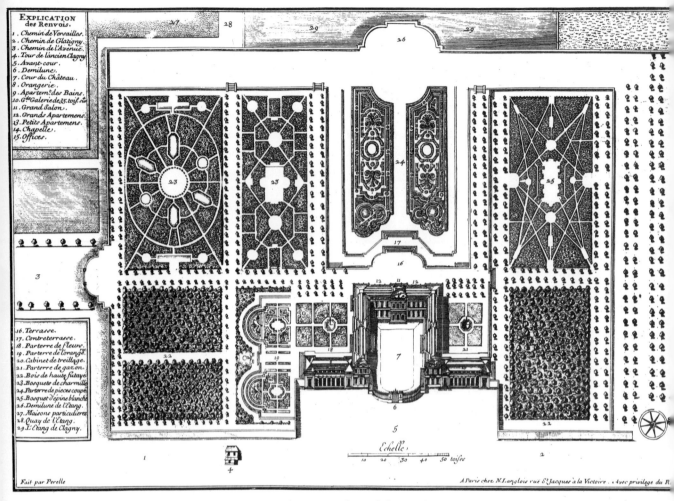

EXPLICATION
des Renvois.
1. Chemin de Versailles.
2. Chemin de Glatigny.
3. Chemin de l'Avenue.
4. Tour de l'ancien Clagny.
5. Avant-cour.
6. Demilune.
7. Cour du Château.
8. Orangerie.
9. Apartem.t des Bains.
10. G.de Galerie de 35. toif. ou
11. Grand Salon.
12. Grands Apartemens.
13. Petits Apartemens.
14. Chapelle.
15. Offices.

16. Terrasse.
17. Contreterrasse.
18. Parterre de fleurs.
19. Parterre de l'orangé.
20. Cabinet de treillage.
21. Parterre de gazon.
22. Bois de haute futaye.
23. Bosquets de charmille.
24. Parterre de pieces coupé.
25. Bosquet d'épine blanche.
26. Demilune de l'etang.
27. Maisons particulieres.
28. Quay de l'Etang.
29. L'Etang de Clagny.

Fait par Perelle

Echelle
10   20   30   40   50 toises

A Paris chez N. Langlois rue S.t Jacques à la Victoire . Avec privilege du R.

Clagny. A plan of the gardens.

herself a heroine in a Corneille tragedy. Louis never fully forgave her for siding against him during the Fronde and it was said by some that he intentionally prevented her from making a suitable marriage. She was either incapable of understanding his attitude toward her, or she pretended to be, for she loved life at court and spent most of her time there.

The following story shows how much Le Nôtre was esteemed by the King, how sure he was of himself, and how he could be entirely natural without creating an embarrassing situation. After she had bought the property

150

of Choisy, two leagues from Paris, *La Grande Mademoiselle* writes in her diary:

> *I purchased it for 40,000 livres and took Le Nôtre to see it but he said that it would first be necessary to cut down most of the woods. The suggestion to cut down the few trees standing there displeased me for I like to stroll at all hours. Le Nôtre told the King I had chosen the worst situation in the world and that the river could be seen only from a dormer window. When I went to court a few days later, very happy about my property, the King asked so many questions about it that this pleased me greatly; and after having let me tell him all about it, he told me what Le Nôtre had said.*

Many years later the Duchess fell in love with and married the Comte de Lauzun. He persuaded his wife it would be politic to ask Le Nôtre, so high in favor, to design her garden. Without mentioning Le Nôtre she described her garden in her diary, "There is an orangerie, a vegetable garden and three fountains and everything is in harmony with the beauty of my house which has grandeur though it is so small."

It is curious that within a hundred years the house and garden at Montmorency should have been the much-loved home of two people of such opposite ideas about art and life as Charles Le Brun, the King's classical artist-decorator, and Jean-Jacques Rousseau, guiding spirit of the Romantic movement. For Rousseau who worshiped nature untouched and unchanged by man, was enthusiastic about the classical house and garden designed by Le Brun and Le Nôtre. In the second volume of his *Confessions*, Rousseau speaks of the skill and artistry shown by Le Nôtre in this architectural garden:

> *The park and garden of Montmorency is not as level as that of La Chevrette. It is uneven, hilly, mingled with heights and depressions which the clever artist used to vary the woods, the water and views, and to enlarge, so to speak, a fairly limited place by art and genius. The park is crowned by the terrace and the château; below, it forms a gorge which opens and widens toward the valley and is filled with a large pool. Between the orangerie [built after Le Brun's time] which occupies a wide area, and the water surrounded by*

slopes decorated with groves and trees, is the little château I mentioned. This edifice and the land around it formerly belonged to the famous Le Brun who delighted in building, and decorated it with the exquisite taste for ornament and architecture for which he was known. The château has since been rebuilt but on the plan of the first master. It is small, simple but elegant. When one looks at this building from the opposite height, which gives it a perspective, it seems as completely environed by water as if it were on an enchanted island, the prettiest of the three islands of the Borromeos, called Isola Bella, in Lago Maggiore.

This is an apt comparison, for Isola Bella was originally a flat island and had been built up into a hill by means of manmade terraces.

Colbert hesitated a long time before he agreed to spend the sums required to build a home appropriate to his exalted position among the ministers of Louis XIV. He had a sense of guilt about this because it was he who had been instrumental in bringing about the downfall of Fouquet. However, by 1670 he had been in power nineteen year and the memories of his role in that scandal had grown so faint that he purchased the barony of Sceaux, an estate seven and a half miles north of Paris.

One of Colbert's duties was to supervise all expenses and to disburse pensions to artists in France as well as abroad. Therefore, he knew better than anyone else who were the ablest of all the artists who worked for the King, and it is noteworthy that he chose Perrault for his architect, Le Brun for his decorator and painter, Girardon and Coysevox for his sculptors, and Le Nôtre for his garden architect.

Work was begun on the grounds in 1673. The land was very uneven and required a great deal of grading. This was so expensive that the plan was not carried out in its entirety during Colbert's lifetime but was completed after his death by his son, the marquis de Seignelay. In order to avoid the vexations at Versailles caused by the inadequate water supply, Colbert had a reservoir built to collect nearby streams and springs.

Le Nôtre felt he must create a most unusual garden if it were to be in keeping with Colbert's taste and position. When it was finished Sceaux was superb. He placed the house at one end of the property in order to leave the largest possible area to be landscaped. The entrance led through a forecourt following the conventional pattern. The central axis passed through the center of the house and continued as a walk to an open terrace facing west and down steps between a *parterre de broderie* and other parterres. The original plan was to have two parallel *allées* south of the terraces and at right angles to the central vista. They were called the *Allée des Cascades* and the *Grand Canal*.

The first of these to be made was the *Allée des Cascades*. (Later it was called the *Allée de la Duchesse*, when Sceaux became the property of the Duchesse de Maine, granddaughter of the Grand Condé and wife of the son of Louis XIV and Madame de Montespan.) This *allée* has been described as a river of stone between rows of trees. The "river" was a cascade tumbling down the hill from one step to the next, terminating in a terrace on the south side of the house. Along the banks were bronze vases spurting water and statues of tigers, lions and panthers that spat water into the foaming torrent. At its far end the waters poured into a huge octagonal basin rimmed with marble and called *mare morte*. However, the waters were not silent for in the center rose a single huge jet.

The second important feature, the *Grand Canal* west of the *Allée de la Duchesse*, was not executed until after Colbert's death. It consisted of a stately body of water, two-thirds of a mile long. To offset its feeling of narrowness, a rounded basin was set halfway down it's length, the margins broken by angles. A narrow watercourse connected the *Grand Canal* with the octagon of the *Allée des Cascades*.

Perrault's work here was fine. Two pavilions at the entrance, the orangerie, and the *Pavilion d'Aurore*, all decorated by Le Brun, are still standing, but the house has disappeared. Sceaux now belongs to the State and restoration was begun under Monsieur Forestier's direction in the early 1930's.

Colbert lived quietly at Sceaux, for when he went there he wanted to relax from his arduous life at court. He did not welcome strangers who came to see the place. There is a story that one day when Boileau and Racine were visiting him, a certain bishop came to call. When he was announced, Colbert told his maître d'hôtel, "Let him be shown everything except me."

CHAPTER XIII

TRIANON:
A NEW SPIRIT
IN THE GARDEN

ANDRÉ LE NÔTRE in his late seventies was as alert and almost as busy as in the early days of his fame. It was at this time that he achieved a garden which, more then any of his others, pointed toward the future. This was because of its simplicity, away from crowds and glitter; it was a place for relaxation.

After creating and supervising at Versailles for thirty years, he had seen his King achieve his aim, to build a capital for France which would surpass in grandeur any in Europe. In the 1690's, he saw Louis, now in his fifties, becoming bored with it. Louis was turning against these stilted court ceremonies he had once insisted upon. At times it seemed that he could hardly endure the great palace crowded with thousands of guests and servants. He wanted a place where he could relax from his pose as The Sun King.

So he chose a little building, situated at the northern end of the *Grand Canal*, opposite the Managery which was placed at the southern end. Built a few years after work began at Versailles, it had been intended as a garden house, and had a one-story main building with four smaller buildings near it. Louis commissioned Mansart and de Cotte to plan a new building for the same site, and called on the aged Le Nôtre to design the gardens.

The building that had been on the site had been designed by Le Vau and had been known as *Le Trianon de Porcelaine*. Shortly before it was built in 1670, Jesuit missionaries had returned from a mission to China combining religion with a hope of increasing French trade. One result was the introduction of Chinese lacquers, brocades, and porcelains into France. These exquisite arts of old China were acclaimed with enthusiasm and were widely copied.

Le Vau thought his new Trianon had "a Chinese elevation"; actually, it was an Italian Renaissance building with Chinese embellishments. It was faced with blue and white Delft tiles and decorated with porcelain figures and vases. To harmonize with the building, the pools and pots in the garden were all made of real or imitation porcelain.

The house and garden created a sensation and became known as the *Trianon de Porcelaine*. However, after seventeen years Louis tired of his *Trianon de Porcelaine*. It had served his purpose in becoming the talk of Europe; so he had it demolished. Mansart and Robert de Cotte were commissioned to plan a new building for the same spot. It had one story with two pavilions connected by a colonnade and was called *Trianon de Flore*. The north wing, projecting into woods, was called *Trianon-sous-Bois*. The gardens laid out for the first Trianon were changed very little. The new name, *Trianon de Flore*, was particularly appropriate because effects in the garden were contrived more from horticultural material than from architectural features. There were quantities of flowers, *bosquets*, old-time bowers, and little rills of water flowing around trees, all features which were to become prominent in the romantic garden of the next century.

The gardens here have been erroneously attributed to Michel Le Bouteux (a nephew and assistant of Le Nôtre) and his father, who were two of the most expert flower gardeners of their time. But a manuscript found by Ragnar Josephson in 1927 in the archives of the National Museum in Stockholm contains correspondence between the Swedish architect Nicodème Tessin and Le Nôtre which proves that Le Nôtre was their author. Young Le Bouteux had made a model of the gardens in wood; after this had been carried out, he was put in charge of them. His father, too, worked there and invented the immense, greatly admired greenhouse in the second parterre, a movable structure of glass supported by wooden frames. It was intended as a cover for the orange trees, jasmine, heliotrope, tuberoses, and other delicate

Trianon. The château and parterre. An engraving by Rigaud.

plants; they could thus be grown in the ground and kept out-of-doors all winter instead of having to be put into pots and brought indoors.

Through the fortunate discovery of Nicodème Tessin's manuscript, it is possible to read a description by Le Nôtre of one of his own gardens. By the time he wrote this Le Nôtre was a delightful old gentleman of eighty. With his usual amiability he took the time and pains to comply with the request for a plan of the Trianon to be given to the Swedish Ambassador to France. Age had not impaired his dexterity in drawing. The plan was executed with the firmness of a young hand, in Chinese ink and in green, blue, and brown wash. However, the handwriting in the description that accompanies the plan is shaky. (His natural medium of expression was drawing; he seldom used handwriting and evidently not with facility.) In all of Le Nôtre's writings the spelling is erratic and the language awkward but his enthusiasm sparkled as he wrote:

Two streams run along a wide alley bordered with large trees and with a palisade made of yew, which terminates in two cascades and form the finest and most sombre allée and has a gentle slope; the cascade close to the apartment furnishes the water for the one at the end of the fine allée.

There are fountains all along the apartment of Trianon-sous-Bois. Here the length and width is filled with high woods in which the trees are separated from each other; in the empty spaces around the trees are little canals which twist and turn unequally. All the canals are separated and one falls into the next through an almost imperceptible slope of the whole wood. On the two sides in the wood are little waterfalls and in them jets of water rise twelve feet high and end in two whirlpools which are then lost in the ground.

Words fail in describing the beauty of this spot; it is so cool that the ladies come here to work, play and eat, and it is very beautiful; one enters on the level of one apartment; then from this apartment one goes under cover to all the beauties of the different allées, thickets, woods of the whole covered garden. I can say it is the only garden, this one and the Tuileries, which I know to be easy to walk in and most beautiful; I leave the others in their beauty and grandeur, but this one is more comfortable.

Writing of the elaborate use of water he speaks of

a garden which is a boulingrin (a parterre with grass) with the design of grass plots surrounded by an allée composed of elms and hornbeams which in turn are outside the streams of water that encircle the enclosure . . . filled with countless jets of water spaced equally, twelve feet apart . . . From above and in the center of all these the waters fall in twenty-three sheets, three feet wide and as high as the bank.

Farther along he speaks of a place where a building is set on a terrace reached by seven steps, "which raise the said building and make it beautiful." There were two fine arbors of jasmine of an admirable beauty and "a fine wood of which the central *allée* makes an admirable vault fifty feet high, where the sun never enters nor does it in any part of the wood." Of another spot he says, "This is one of the most beautiful parts of the garden, for one sees the *allée* or the center of the wood, which appears to be a vault covered with woods of great height, and one sees the arcades of the peristyle of the palace."

Le Nôtre ends his letter in words revealing his charm; he says that, though proud of his work, he regards it almost as if it were something apart from himself, and he describes himself as a humble gardener. He writes, "There, Monsieur, you have what I have tried to explain as best I could so that the plan will be intelligible to you and that you will be informed. Excuse my lack of knowledge and my discourse, which I give you as it is. I took a lot of pains and it was more difficult for me to write than to make this plan." He hints ingenuously at receiving medals for his collection in recompense for his work: "I beg you to show the plan to *Monsieur l'Ambassadeur* and assure him of my service. When you have need, command me and also if you have any new medals, let me know for I have many; you must let me know."

The spirit motivating the Trianon gardens was new because Le Nôtre wanted them to contrast with the formality of the gardens of the court; in its attempt to be natural it foretold the romantic style. Yet Le Nôtre was so much a man of his time, and his idiom so distinctly of the seventeenth century, that the over-all effect remained classical. One feels the new spirit in his use of materials, in his adaptation to the existing woods, and, above all, in his own words, the fact that "this (garden) is more comfortable."

It took another hundred years before men would be sufficiently free and secure not to feel they must discipline nature, before they would encourage trees to spread to their full breadth and shrubs to grow in whatever form was natural to them. Yet the idea expressed by Le Nôtre at the Trianon long anticipated this turning toward a more tolerant and relaxed view of life. Like all true artists, he both interpreted the spirit of his time and was a prophet of the future.

It was while the second building at the Trianon was going up that there occurred a much-discussed incident which involved a defect in a casement and revealed Le Nôtre's extraordinary tact. The story is taken from the *Journal* of Philippe de Dangeau, a courtier with a literary flair.

"The King had an extraordinary eye for exactitude, proportion and symmetry though his taste was not on the same high level. On his visit to Trianon the King noted a fault in one of the casements of a window on the ground floor and spoke of this to Louvois who, in addition to numerous other duties, had succeeded Colbert as *intendent de bâtiments*. This minister was rude and spoiled; he did not suffer correction from his master, but argued strongly and loudly, maintaining that the casement was right. The King turned his back and walked elsewhere in the building. The next day he came upon Monsieur Le Nôtre, famous for his taste in French gardens, where his designs reach the highest point of perfection, and also a good architect. The King asked him whether he had been to Trianon, and when Le Nôtre answered 'No,' the King explained to him what he had noticed and ordered him to go to see it for himself. The next day the same question and the same answer, and the day after as well. The King realized perfectly that Le Nôtre did not wish to show that Monsieur Louvois was in the wrong. He grew angry and commanded Le Nôtre to be there the next day when he would come to Trianon in the course of his promenade. After this it was not possible to evade the question and Monsieur Le Nôtre met the King and Louvois at the Trianon. Immediately the subject of the window came up. Monsieur de Louvois argued and Le Nôtre said not a word. Finally the King ordered Le Nôtre to measure and align the casement and report on what he found. While Le Nôtre was working Louvois was furious and kept scolding and insisting the window was exactly like the other six. All this time the King was silent. Le Nôtre began to stammer and the King became angry and commanded him to speak out; then Le Nôtre admitted the King was right and said he had found a mistake. He had hardly finished when the King turned to Louvois and said he could not stand his obstinacy; that if he had not noticed the window was crooked it would have been built that way and the whole building would have had to be torn down as soon as it had been finished. In other words he reprimanded Louvois soundly."

CHAPTER XIV

OLD AGE
WITH HONORS

A NDRÉ LE NÔTRE had lived an active outdoor life and been a man of moderate, sober habits; he kept his strength and creative capacities and continued to work, though not with the same intensity, to the end of his long life. After his seventy-seventh year, he relinquished a good part of his work at Versailles to others, particularly to Mansart, but he seems to have retained his position as super. intendent of buildings until two years before his death.

Louis de Bachaumont, who was brought up in an apartment adjoining that of Le Nôtre, in the building (called *le Grand Commun*) opposite the south wing of the palace at Versailles, wrote of the old garden architect: "He was the pleasantest old gentleman that ever was, always jolly, clean, and well dressed. He had an agreeable expression and was always laughing." He told how Le Nôtre entertained him when he was a little boy by drawing funny figures "with an inconceivable rapidity" and how the old artist encouraged the boy's first attempts at drawing.

In 1694, at eighty-one years, Le Nôtre wrote a letter to Monsieur de Pontchartrain in which he mentions having finished the design for his garden. Other documents show him to have been concerned at that time with the plans his nephew, Claude Desgots, was to take to England; in the same year he made the drawings and wrote the description of the Trianon for Nicodème Tessin.

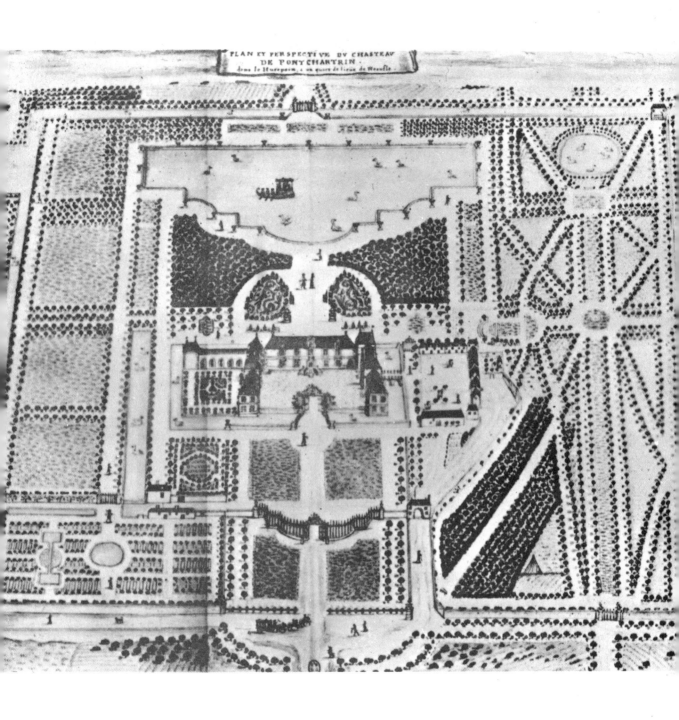

Pontchartrain. Plan for the gardens, among the last designed by Le Nôtre.

Two years later, he wrote a letter to Monsieur de Gaude which shows how active he still was as superintendent of buildings:

> *I beg you, Monsieur, to have the kindness to give me an hour of your time tomorrow. I will come for you and we will go together in a carriage to see a house close to the Luxembourg, where a wall overlooking the garden fell down and was rebuilt, to find out if it was rebuilt to the correct height and if it is out of line or unlike its neighbors in order to report to Monsieur the superintendent, since I wish to have it exactly right. I will take you back to wherever you would like to go since you are one of my friends and I should like to oblige you without any other reward than that of pleasing you. A little word of response would oblige me, Monsieur.*
>
> > *Your very obedient servitor*
> > *Le Nôtre.*

Le Nôtre continued active with respect to his art collection and kept adding to his medals. Dr. Lister expressed an opinion, widely held in Paris at the time, when he wrote:

> *Monsieur Le Nôtre's rooms wherein he keeps his fine things were worth seeing. He is a very ingenious old gentleman and the planning and designing of most of the royal and great gardens in and about Paris have been his work and he has lived to see them in perfection. This gentleman is in his late eighties and quick and lively. He entertained me very civilly. . . . The French King has a particular kindness for him; he is much delighted with his humor and will sit and look at his medals and when he comes to any medals that are against the King, Le Nôtre will say, "Sire, here is one which is against us."*

Being meticulous, Le Nôtre made careful plans about the disposition of his art collection. Monsieur de Seignelay, Colbert's son, who was rapidly dissipating his father's fortune, offered Le Nôtre eighty thousand *livres* for certain items of his collection and was refused. Before Le Nôtre's day, noblemen and statesmen had frequently returned a goodly part of their fortunes to the throne. In this tradition, in the year 1693, the gardener invited the King to come to his house to select any items he desired. The King chose twenty paintings, among them three by Poussin and two by Claude Lorraine; bronzes including Michaelangelo's *Captive* and a statue by Michel Anguier; nine marbles, two vases, eight busts and six pedestals. It was estimated that these items were worth about one hundred and fifty thousand *livres*. In appreciation the King granted Le Nôtre a pension of six thousand *livres*. The paintings were placed in a small gallery of the King's apartment; the statues and vases were disposed about the royal gardens.

It must have pleased Le Nôtre to know his finest pieces were henceforth part of the royal collections. Some of his paintings are in the Museum of the Louvre today. The *Mercure de France*, newspaper of the day, in writing of the gift expresses the pride felt by the public that one of them, a man who began as a gardener, should become such a Maecenas. It said that the art objects "lost nothing of their beauty through being put along with all that is finest in Europe."

In February of 1700, Le Nôtre, always a careful *bourgeois*, went to his notary to dictate and sign his will. Although the occasion was solemn, he put in a joke about how careful his wife had been with his money and how she had rather he would save than spend it on works of art. Madame Le Nôtre was to be his executrix, with the Sieur de Reddemont, his brother-in-law, to help her.

The inventory of Le Nôtre's estate indicates what a luxurious home he had and how magnificently it was furnished. Besides the works of art, there were wall tapestries, embroidered linen hangings at the window, copper vessels in the kitchen, and Madame Le Nôtre's white satin dressing table, her jewels and fine dresses. There were coffers filled with nineteen bags of gold and silver pieces (Le Nôtre was prepared for any emergency) and superb silver vessels for the table. From motives of economy, he had not had his silver melted when the King and others had done so.

In his will, Le Nôtre left money to his valet and his old servant, Marie. There is a glimpse of his social circle through the other bequests. To his cousin, Suzanne Leroy, to her younger sister, his great-nieces and nephews, and several widows he left pensions and money. To his friend, Le Sieur Rousset, he left a copy of his portrait and a black suit for mourning in case he should care to wear it for him. A gold chain, perhaps the one given him by the King of England, was to be sold for cash to gild the silver cross he had given to the Church of Saint-Roch, and, "if he had it gilded during his lifetime, to make an epitaph on a black marble table in letters of gold."

He indicated that he wanted to die as he had been born, as a gardener, requesting that he "be buried in the Chapel of Saint-André, erected in the Church of Saint-Roch, with the least possible ceremony, nor should he be given the title of gentleman . . . nor also in the vault of the same Chapel should anyone else but him, the Lady his wife and the Lady de Reddemont, be buried." Masses were ordered for his soul and money was to be distributed to the poor after the burial ceremonies.

There is a last picture of the King and his gardener, typical of the best of Louis and of their relationship. On a sunny day in July only a month before his death, Le Nôtre went to visit the gardens at Versailles. The King, who had been expecting him, welcomed him with delight. With his habitual tact, Louis, now also getting on in years and no longer able to travel through the vast gardens on foot, invited the old gardener to step into a wheel chair, like the one he used, and be pushed alongside him.

Riding at the King's side, unaware that this was to be his last garden tour, Le Nôtre must have let his thoughts wander over his life, as old people do. He would have remembered his joy when the garden at Versailles was finished, long ago: the great fêtes he had seen in his enclosed *bosquets*, the day when the fountains first were turned on at Versailles, that momentous party forty years before at Vaux; and himself as a boy, working in the Tuileries gardens beside his father. How carefully he had been educated! His father and all the family and their friends had predicted a fine future for him, but none of them could have dreamed it would be as brilliant as it was.

After some such thought, legend tells us that he suddenly exclaimed to the King, "Ah, my poor father! If he were alive and could see a poor gardener like his son, riding in a chair beside the greatest king in the world, my joy would be complete!"

Le Nôtre died in Paris, at four o'clock in the morning of September 15, 1700. With him were a priest of the parish of Saint-Germain-l'Auxerrois; his wife; Le Sieur de Reddemont; Nicolas Bernau, an equerry; and Armand-Claude Mollet, who had married his niece and was one of his assistants.

The Mercure de France carried this notice of his death:

The King has lost a rare man, zealous for his service and very distinguished in the art to which he brought honor. This is Monsieur Le Nôtre, Superintendent of his Majesty's Buildings and Gardens and of the Arts and Manufactures of France. The King had honored him with the Order of Saint-Michel, to mark the esteem and distinction he felt for him. No man has ever known better than he everything which contributes to the beauty of gardens, and even Italy acknowledges this. To be aware of his great knowledge it is only necessary to cast one's eyes upon the gardens at Versailles and the Tuileries and it is impossible to withhold the admiration his work inspires. He did not leave as much shade in the gardens he designed as certain people would have liked but he could not bear a circumscribed view and did not think fine gardens should resemble forests. He was esteemed by all the sovereigns in Europe and there are few who have not requested the design of a garden from him.

Le Nôtre composed his own epitaph, a frank and direct piece of writing. As in his will, it is evident that to him worldly honors and distinctions were not to be compared with the transcendence of his genius, which he always regarded as something God-given or outside himself. He wanted to be known to posterity as a gardener who was supreme in his work, unrivaled in the whole world. He felt his work expressed the greatness of the monarch whom he admired and loved, and he wanted posterity to know how well that monarch had treated him.

ICI REPOSE LE CORPS D'ANDRÉ LE NÔTRE,

CHEVALIER DE L'ORDRE DE SAINT-MICHEL, CONSEILLER DU ROI,

CONTRÔLEUR GÉNÉRAL DES BÂTIMENTS DE SA MAJESTÉ,

ARTS ET MANUFACTURES DE FRANCE,

ET PRÉPOSÉ À L'EMBELLISHEMENT DES JARDINS DE VERSAILLES ET

AUTRES MAISONS ROYALES.

LA FORCE ET L'ÉTENDUE DE SON GÉNIE

LE RENDAIENT SI SINGULIER DANS L'ART DE JARDINAGE,

QU'ON PEUT LE REGARDER COMME EN AYANT INVENTÉ LES

BEAUTÉS PRINCIPALES,

ET PORTÉ TOUTES LES AUTRES À LEUR DERNIÈRE PERFECTION.

IL RÉPONDIT EN QUELQUE SORTE, PAR L'EXCELLENCE DE SES
OUVRAGES,

À LA GRANDEUR ET À LA MAGNIFICENCE DU MONARQUE QU'IL
A SERVI

ET DONT IL A ÉTÉ COMBLÉ DE BIENFAITS.

LA FRANCE N'A PAS SEULE PROFITÉ DE SON INDUSTRIE,

TOUS LES PRINCES DE L'EUROPE ONT VOULU AVOIR DE SES
ÉLÈVES

ET IL N'A POINT EU DE CONCURRENT QUI LUI FÛT COMPARABLE.

IL NACQUIT EN L'ANNÉE 1613

ET MOURUT DANS LE MOIS DE SEPTEMBRE D' L'ANNÉE 1700 *

* Here lies the body of André Le Nôtre, chevalier of the Order of Saint-Michel, Councillor of the King, Superintendent of Royal Buildings and Arts and Manufactures of France, and Superintendent of the embellishment of the gardens at Versailles and other royal dwellings. The force and scope of his genius made him so outstanding in the art of gardening that he can be regarded as having invented their principal beauties and carried all others to their utmost perfection. The excellence of his work accorded with the grandeur and magnificence of the monarch he served and by whom he was showered with benefactions. Not only did France profit from his industry but all the princes of Europe sought his pupils. He had no comparable rival. He was born in 1613 and died in September 1700.

APPENDIX

Gardens originated or remade by Le Nôtre, and those in which he may have worked as a young man.

Anet. Eure-et-Loire. Le Nôtre remade a portion.

Aux Enfants Trouvés. Paris.

Bellegarde. In Gatinais park, Seine-et-Oise. Guiffrey believes this is the work of Le Nôtre.

Beloiel, Belgium.

Bercy. Château on the right bank of the Seine near Paris.

Blois. Le Nôtre worked here, but did not originate the gardens.

Boucheret. Paris.

Bouillon, Hôtel de. Parterre.

Bourges. Parc de L'Archevêché.

Bushy Hill Park, England.

Carday. Auvergne.

Carnaback. Côtes-du-Nord.

Castries. Hérault.

Chabrillon. Near Saint Vallier.

Chamalieres. Near Rogat.

Chantilly.

Château de la Planche. Near Villedieu du Clair, Vienne. Destroyed during the Revolution.

Château-neuf-sur-Loire. Loiret.

✓Chatsworth, Derbyshire, England.

Chaville. Near Versailles, Seine-et-Oise. Belonged to Le Tellier, Chancellor of France; finished *ca.* 1660.

Chesnay. Seine-et-Oise.

Choisy-le-Roi.

Clagny. Near Versailles. No longer exists.

Claire. Jardin de Claire. Near Lyons.

Clayes. May be near Versailles.

Condé, Hôtel de. Paris.

Conflans. Paris. Destroyed.

Cordes. 30 km from Claremont. Famous charmille (hedge of hornbean).

Courances. On the way to Fontainebleau. Restored by Duchesne.

Cramaye-en-Brie. Belonged to President Mesmes.

Dampierre. Near Versailles, in the valley of the Chevreuse.

Dijon. Part of the city. May have been designed by a pupil named Dimarche Prunard; Guiffrey believes Le Nôtre designed the public gardens, created under the princes of Condé, governors of Bourgoyne.

√Fontainebleau. The parterre of the Tiber.

Gaillon. Near Rouen. Le Nôtre worked here.

√Greenwich Park, England.

Hautoie. Near Amiens.

Issy. Near Paris.

Jardin des Incurables. Paris.

Kassel. Germany. For the Landgraf of Hesse.

Kerjean. Brittany. Now national property.

La Planche. Near Villedieu-du-clain, Vienne.

Les Rochers. Brittany. For the Marquise de Sévigné.

Liancourt. Oise. And a house in Paris belonging to Salomon de Brosse.

Liancourt. On rue de Seine, Paris.

Livry.

Louvois, Hôtel de. Parterre de broderie. Near Rheims.

Louvois. House in Paris.

Luxembourg. Paris.

Maintenon. Southwest of Paris.

Maisons. Paris. For René de Longuiel.

Marsan. Hôtel de. Paris. Parterre.

Meaux. Garden of Séguier and Bossuet.

Meudon. Near Paris. No longer exists.

Montdétour. Vexin.

Montjeu. Near Autun.

Montjolly. Auvergne.

Montmorency. En route to Fontainebleau.

Noisy-le-Roy. Seine-et-Oise.

Ognen. Near Senlis.

Pamphili and Ludovisi gardens. Italy.

Pantin. Park, destroyed in the Revolution.

Petit Bourg. For Duc D'Antin.

Pinon. Aisne.

Pomponne. Seine-et-Marne.

Pontchartrain. In the Hurepoix near Heauflé.

Pragney. Canton de Longeau. Haute-Marne. Destroyed.

Raincy. House built before 1650 by Le Vau for Bordier, *intendant des finances*. Blomfield
   is certain that Le Nôtre did the gardens.

Rambouillet. Seine-et-Oise.

Rueil. John Evelyn says it was a league from St. Germain.

Park of Madame de la Sablière, Normandie.

Saint-Cloud. Outside Paris.

Saint-Germain. Outside Paris. Parterres.

√St. James Park. London, England.

Saint-Maur. Indre-et-Loire. Gardens designed by Le Nôtre, probably before 1670.

Saint-Poange, Hôtel rue des Petits Champs. Paris.

Sceaux. Outside Paris. For Colbert.

Seilleraye. Near Nantes.

Thoiry. Near Versailles.

Tuileries. First work.

Trianon. At Versailles.

Valgenceuse. An old fief. Le Nôtre is said to have been called in when he was at Chantilly.

Vaux-le-Vicomte. Near Melun.

Versailles.

Vic-sur-Aisne. Between Compiègne and Seissons. Built by Abbé de Pomponeme toward the end of Louis XIV's reign; sculpture by Coustou and Coysevox.

Villedieu-du-Clain. In Vienne.

Villes-Cotterets. Ile de France. Le Nôtre may have remade gardens.

Vincennes. Outside Paris. Gardens and terraces.

Whitehall Park. London.

Wideville. Seine-et-Oise. For Claude de Boullion.

BIBLIOGRAPHY

CONTEMPORARY SOURCES

Androuet du Cerceau, Jacques. *French Châteaux and Gardens in the XVIth Century*. With an account of the artist and his work, by W. H. Ward. London: B. T. Batsford, 1909.

——. Le Premier-Second volume; *Les plus excellents bastiments de France*. Paris: 1576-79; nouv. ed., Paris: A. Levy, 1868-70.

Aviler, Augustin Charles d'. *Cours d'architecture*. Paris: N. Langlois, 1691; nouv. ed., Paris: J. Mariette, 1738.

Blondel, Jacques François. *Architecture à la Mode*. Manuscript in the Bibliothèque Nationale, Paris, 2 vols.

——. *Architecture françoise*. 4 vols. Paris: C. A. Jombert, 1752-56.

——. *Cours d'architecture*. 6 vols. Paris: Dessaint, 1771-77.

——. *De la distribution des maisons de plaisance*. 2 vols. Paris: C. A. Jombert, 1737-38.

Boyceau, Jacques Seigneur de la Barauderie: *Traité du jardinage selon les raisons de la nature et de l'art*. Paris: M. Vanlochom, 1638.

Catalogue d'exposition retrospective de l'art des jardins en France du XVIe siècle à la fin du XVIIIe. Palais du Louvre, Pavillon de Marsan, mai-octobre, 1913. To celebrate the threehundredth anniversary of Le Nôtre's birth.

Dezallier d'Argenville, Antoine Joseph. *La théorie et la pratique du jardinage*. Paris: J. Mariette, 1709. First edition was published under the initials L.S.A.J.D.A.; second under the name Alexandre Le Blond.

——. *The Theory and Practice of Gardening*. London: G. James, 1712. A translation of the above.

——. *Vies des Fameux Architectes*. Paris: Debure, 1787.

——. *Voyage pittoresque de Paris*. 6 ed. Paris: de Bure, 1785.

Duhamel du Monceau, Henri Louis. *A Practical Treatise of Husbandry*. Translated by John Mills. London: C. Hitch and L. Hawes, 1762.

Estienne, Charles, and Liébault, Jean. *Maison rustique, or The Countrie Farme*. Translated by Richard Surflet. London, 1600. Published in Latin with title *Praedium Rusticum*. Lutetiae: C. Stephanum, 1554. In French *L'agriculture et maison rustique*. Paris: Du Puis, 1570.

Félibien, André. *Description sommaire du chasteau de Versailles*. Paris: G. Desprez, 1674.

——. *Relation de la feste de Versailles du 18e juillet*. Paris: P. Le Petit, 1668. Also Paris: L'Imp. Royale, 1679.

Josephson, Ragnar. *Le grand Trianon sous Louis XIV*. In *Revue de l'histoire de Versailles*, 1927, pp. 5-20.

La Brosse, Guy de. *Description du jardin royal.* Paris, 1636. Lists of plants according to their uses.

La Chesnée Monstereul, Charles de. *Le floriste françois.* Caen: E. Mangeant, 1654. About the tulip mania of 1634-37.

La Quintinie, Jean de. *Instructions pour les jardins fruitiers et potagers.* Paris: C. Barbin, 1690. John Evelyn's translation has title *The Compleat Gard'ner*, editions of 1699 and 1701.

Le Bouteux, Michel, fils. *Plan et dessins nouveaux du jardinie.* Paris, 1780.

Le Nôtre, André. "Description du Grand Trianon en 1694." In *Revue de L'Histoire de Versailles*, 1926, pp. 20-23.

Le Pautre, Pierre. *Descriptions de Versailles et de ses dependances.* Paris: Demortain, 1717. A good plan and thirtyfour plates.

————. Engravings of the Berceau de treillage près du labyrinthe à Versailles.

Liger, Louis, sieur d'Auxerre. *Le jardinier fleuriste et historiographe.* Paris: D. Beugnié, 1704.

Ligne, Charles Joseph, Prince de. *Coup d'œil sur Belœil et sur une grande partie des jardins de l'Europe.* Nouv. éd. Bruxelles: F. Hayet, 1786. A reproduction was published in Paris: Bossard, 1922.

Mariette. Published plates of Versailles, Clagny, Sceaux, etc., in one volume. At the Sign of the Column of Hercules. He was grandfather of the following:

Mariette, Pierre Jean. *Abecedario.* Paris: J. B. Dumoulin, 1853-62.

————. *Architecture à la mode, où sont les nouveaux dessins pour la decoration des bâtiments et jardins.* 3 vols. Paris: N. Langlois.

————. *L'Architecture française.* Paris, 1727. A reproduction was published Paris: G. Vanest, 1927; edited by Louis Hautecouer in 6 vols.

Marot, Jean. *Architectural plans.* 2 vols. Paris, ca. 1727.

Marot, L. *Dessins.*

Mercure Galant, 1686, 2. partie, pp. 210-13. Description of Versailles with an account of the visit of ambassadors from Siam.

Mollet, André. *Le jardin de plaisir.* Stockholm: H. Kayser, 1651.

Mollet, Claude. *Théâtre des plants et jardinages.* Paris: C. de Sercy, 1652.

Palissy, Bernard. *A Delectable Garden.* Translated with an introduction by Helen Morgenthau Fox. Peekskill, New York: The Watch Hill Press, 1931.

Passe, Crispinjn van de. *Hortus Floridus.* London: The Cresset Press, 1928-29. Comprises the first book only of the *Hortus Floridus* as published originally in 1615.

Perelle, Gabriel. Engravings.

Perelle, Adam, and others. *Divers vues et perspectives des fontaines et jardins de Fontaine-bel-eau et autres lieux.*

Rigaud, Jean. *Recueil choisie des plus belles vues de palaces, châteaux, maisons de plaisances, etc. de Paris, et de ses environs.* Paris, 1752.

Serres, Olivier de, seigneur du Pradel. *Le théâtre d'agriculture et mesnage des champs.* Paris, 1600.

Silvestre, Israel de. *Jardins et Fontaines.* Paris, 1661.

Tournefort, Joseph Pitton de. *Histoire des plantes qui naissent aux environs de Paris.* Paris: L'Im. Royale, 1698.

Ward, William Henry. *French Châteaux.* See entry under Androuet du Cerceau.

CONTEMPORARY BOOKS ON THE PERIOD

Bossuet, Jacques Bénigne, Bp. of Meaux. *Chefs-d'œuvre de Bossuet. Ses oraisons funèbres.* 2 vols. Paris: F. Didot, 1878.

Bussy-Rabutin, Roger, Comte de. *Mémoires.* Nouv. ed. Paris: Charpentier, 1857.

Caylus, Marthe, Comtesse de. *Souvenirs.* Paris: E. Flammarion, 1882. First published 1770.

Colbert, Jean Baptiste. *The Political Last Testament.* London: R. Bentley, 1695.

———. *Lettres, instructions et mémoires.* Paris: Pierre Clement, 1861-70.

Chantelou, Paul Fréart. "Journal du voyage de cavalier Bernin en France." Ed. by La Laune. *Gazette des Beaux-Arts.* Paris, 1885. Reprint from the *Gazette.* Chantelou accompanied Bernini during his entire stay in France.

Dangeau, Philippe de Courcillon, Marquis de. *Journal, avec les additions du Duc de Saint-Simon.* Paris: F. Didot frères, 1854-60.

Descartes, René. *A Discourse on Method.* Translated by John Veitch. Everyman's Library. London: J. M. Dent, 1924.

Evelyn, John. *Diary.* Akron, Ohio: Dunstan Society, 1901. Covers the years 1641-97.

Fénelon, François de Salignac de la Mothe. *Les aventures de Télémaque.* Paris, 1717.

Haussonville, Gabriel, Comte de, and Hanotaux, G. *Souvenirs sur madame de Maintenon.* Paris: Calmann-Lévy, 1902-4.

Laborde, Léon, Marquis. *Les comptes des bâtiments du roi, 1528-71.* 2 vols. Paris: J. Baur, 1877-80.

La Bruyère, Jean de. *Les caractères.* Paris: Lefèvre, 1918.

La Fayette, Marie, Comtesse de. *Mémoires, précédées de la princesse de Clèves.* Paris: E. Flammarion, 1905.

La Fontaine, Jean de. *Le songe de vaux.*

———. *Fables.*

Ligne, Charles Joseph, Prince de. *Mémoires.* Paris, 1827-29. Author speaks of Clagny and Le Nôtre as favoring Mansart above Le Pautre.

Lister, Martin. *A Journey to Paris in the Year 1698.* London, 1698-99. Reprinted in Pinkerton's *Voyages,* vol. 4. London, 1809.

Louis XIV, King of France. *Oeuvres.* Paris, 1806.

———. *Mémoires.* Paris: Bossard, 1923. Earlier editions: 1767, 1789, and 1806.

Mercure de France, mai 1693, pp. 293-96. Description of Le Nôtre's gift of art treasures to the King.

———. Septembre, 1700, pp. 278-81. Notice of Le Nôtre's death.

Molière, Jean Baptiste Poquelin. *Oeuvres.*

Montpensier, Anne, Duchesse de. *Mémoires, avec notes par A. Chéruel.* Paris: Charpentier, 1858-59.

Motteville, Françoise Bertaut, dame Langlois de. *Mémoires sur Anne d'Autriche et Sacour.* 4 vols. Paris: Charpentier, 1886.

Pascal, Blaise. *Pensées.*

———. Lettres provinciales.

Perrault, Charles. *Les Hommes illustres.* Paris: A. Dezallier, 1696-1700.

———. *Le Siècle de Louis le grand*; poème. Paris: J. B. Coignard, 1687.

Racine, Jean. *Théâtres.*

Retz, Jean François Paul de Gondi, Cardinal de. *Mémoires.* 4 vols. Paris: Garnier, 1935. An English translation was published Philadelphia: Edward Earle, 1817.

Saint-Simon, Louis de Rouvroy, Duc de. *Mémoires sur le règne de Louis XIV et la régence.* Paris: Larousse, 1934.

Scudéry, Madeleine de. *La promenade de Versailles, dédiée au roi.* Embelli d'estampes de Robert Mahias (à l'enseigne du Marque d'Or). Paris: Devambez, 1920. An exquisite little book with colored plates. Reproduction.

Sévigné, Marie, Marquise de. *Lettres choisies.* Paris: Larousse, 1926.

Société de l'Histoire de l'Art Français: *Bulletin*, 1911, pp. 217-82, Le Nôtre's will; pp. 228-35, Catalogue of his effects. Paris.

SOURCES ON LE NÔTRE'S TRIP TO ENGLAND

Warrant from Treasurer, Book X, Oct. 15, 1662, p. 137.

Ward, Cyril. *Royal Gardens.* Longmans.

Walford, Edward, *Old and New London.*

MODERN SOURCES

Babeau, Albert. "Le jardin des Tuileries au XVIIe et au XVIIIe siècle." In, Société de l'Histoire de Paris: *Mémoires*, 28 : 37-66. 1901.

Berty, Adolphe. *Les grands architectes français de la renaissance.* Paris, 1860.

———. *Histoire Générale de Paris.* 6 vols. Paris: Imp. nationale, 1866-97.

———. *Topographie historique du vieux Paris.* 6 vols. Paris: Imp. impériale, 1866-97.

Blomfield, Sir Reginald Theodore. *A History of French Architecture:* from the death of Mazarin till the death of Louis XV, 1661-1774. London: G. Bell, 1921.

Cazes, E. *Le château de Versailles et ses dépendances.* Versailles: L. Bernard, 1910.

Charageat, Marguerite. *L'art des jardins.* Paris: Garnier, 1930.

Charchine, Mlle. B. *Le château de Chorsey.* Paris, 1910.

Le château de Versailles: architecture et decoration. Introd. et notices par G. Brière. 2 vols. Paris: Lib. centrale des beaux-arts, 1913. Brière followed de Nolhac as curator of the museum of Versailles.

Cordey, Jean. Vaux-le-Vicomte. Préface de Pierre de Nolhac. Paris: A. Morancé, 1924.

Corpechot, Lucien. "Les leçons de Versailles et de Saint-Cloud." In *La minèrve Française*, 4: 5-17 (janvier-mars) 1920.

——. *Parcs et jardins de France.* (*Les jardins de l'intelligence.*) Paris: Plon, 1937. One of two modern books on Le Nôtre, and excellent.

Desjardins, Paul. *Poussin.* Paris: H. Laurens, 1903.

Dussieux, Louis Etienne. *Le château de Versailles.* 2 vols. Versailles: L. Bernard, 1881.

Green, Mary Anne Everett. *Calendar of State Papers: Domestic Series of the Reign of Charles II.* London, 1861; pp. 116-62. Preserved in the State Paper Dept. of Her Majesty's Public Record Office.

Fouquier, Marcel. *De L'art des jardins du XVe au XXe siècle.* Paris: E. Paul, 1911.

——. *Les grands châteaux de France.* Préface par M. Pierre de Nolhac. Paris: Imp. Lahure, 1907. Has material on Dampierre.

——, and Duchêne, André. *Des divers styles de jardins.* Paris: E. Paul, 1914. Fine plates.

Gabillot, C. "Pièces inédites concernant André Le Nôtre." In *Revue de l'histoire de Versailles*, 1912, pp. 13-27.

——. "Pièces sur Le Nôtre." In *Gazette des beaux-arts* (avril 1913) 319-32.

Gaignat de l'Aulnais, C. *Promenade de Sceaux-Penthièvre.* Paris: P. F. Gueffier, 1778.

Ganay, Ernest de. *Chantilly au XVIIIe siècle.* Paris: G. Van Oest, 1925.

Girardin, Gernand, Marquis de. *Maisons de plaisance françaises, parcs et jardins, l'île de France.* Paris: A. Morancé, 1920.

Gromort, Georges. *L'Art des jardins.* Paris: Fréal, 1934.

Guiffrey, Jules Marie Joseph. *André Le Nôtre.* Paris: H. Laurens, 1912. One of two books on Le Nôtre, well documented and informative.

Harlay, Charles. *Le Château de Clagny à Versailles.* Versailles: A. Bourdier, 1913.

Houdard, Georges Louis. *Les châteaux royaux de Saint-Germain-en-Laye, 1124-1789.* 2 vols. Saint-Germain-en-Laye: M. Mirvault, 1909-10.

L'Intermédiaire des chercheurs et curieux: Vols. 65-66 (avril 30, mai 10, 30, juillet 10, août, etc., 1912). Lists of châteaux for which Le Nôtre designed the parks.

Josephson, Ragnar. "Le Grand Trianon sous Louis XIV." In *Revue de l'Histoire de Versailles*, 1927, pp. 5-20.

Lery, Edmond. "La Rue et la place Hoche." In *Revue de l'histoire de Versailles*, 1926, pp. 128-43, 264-73.

Massin, Charles (Hector Saint-Sauveur, pseud.). *Les beaux jardins de France.* Paris: C. Massin, 1926.

Nicolle, Henri. *Le château de Maisons.* Paris, 1858.

Nolhac, Pierre de. *L'art de Versailles.* Paris: L. Conrad, 1920.

——. "Les bosquets de Versailles." In *Gazette des beaux arts* (Période 3, 1899-1900), XXII, 265-82, XXIII, 39-54, 283-92.

——. *La création de Versailles.* Versailles: L. Bernard, 1901.

——. *Histoire du château de Versailles.* 2 vols. Paris: A. Marty, 1911.

——. *Les jardins de Versailles.* Paris: Goupil, 1906.

——. *Les Trianons.* Paris: C. Eggimann, 1911.

———. "Trianon de porcelaine." In *Revue de l'histoire de Versailles* 3: 1-16 (février 1901).

———. *Versailles, résidence de Louis XIV.* Paris: L. Conrad, 1925. Nolhac was curator of the museum of Versailles; his books are informative and authoritative and full of allusions to source material.

Le parc de Versailles. Notice par G. Brière. Paris: Lib. Centrale des Beaux-Arts, 1911.

Péan, Prosper. *Jardins de France.* 2 vols. Paris: A. Vincent, 1925. Contains fine photographs of a great many seventeenth century and other châteaux.

Pfnor, Rodolphe. *Le château de Vaux-le-Vicomte.* Texte par Anatole France. Paris: Lemercier, 1888.

———. *Monographie du palais de Fontainbleau.* Paris: A. Morel, 1873.

Richter, Louise Marie. *Chantilly in History and Art.* London: J. Murray, 1913.

Rockley, Alicia Margaret Cecil, Baroness. *A History of Gardening in England.* New York: Dutton, 1910, pp. 192-93.

Stein, Henri. *Les Jardins de France.* Paris: D. A. Longuet, 1913. Has 102 plates and 393 reproductions of old prints, and an excellent bibliography. A most valuable book. The author was assistant curator in the French national archives.

Soulange-Bodin, Henri. *Sceaux, son château, son parc.* Paris: A. Morancé, 1927.

Triggs, Harry Inigo. *Garden Craft in Europe.* London: B. T. Batsford, 1913.

Vacquier, Jules Félix. *Les anciens châteaux de France.* Paris: F. Contet, 1922.

Versailles. *Musée de Versailles et des Trianons.* Catalogue général des galeries historiques. Introd. par J. G. Janin. Paris: C. Gavard, 1846.

Vitry, Paul. *Le château de Maisons-Lafitte.* G. Brown, 1912.

Ward, William Henry. *The Architecture of the Renaissance in France.* New York: Scribner, 1912.

GENERAL SOURCES, NOT CONTEMPORARY

Bertaut, Jean. "Versailles." In *Les Beaux décors littéraires*, VII (octobre-novembre, 1920).

Bertrand, Louis Marie Emile. *Louis XIV.* Paris: Fayard, 1923. Translation, London: Longmans, 1928.

Boulenger, Jacques Romain. *Le grand siècle.* Paris: Hachette, 1915.

Boulenger, Marcel. *Fouquet.* Paris: B. Grasset, 1933.

Chatelain, Urbain Victor. *Le surintendant, Nicholas Foucquet.* Paris: Perrin, 1905.

Funck-Brentano, Frantz. *L'ancien régime.* Paris: D. Fayard, 1926.

———. *L'ancienne France: le roi.* Paris: Hachette, 1930.

———. *Le drame des poisons.* Paris: Hachette, 1906.

Guerard, Albert Léon. *The Life and Death of an Ideal.* New York: Scribner, 1928. Excellent account of the period.

Hallays, André. *Autour de Paris.* 2 vols. Paris: Perrin, 1920-21. Contains a chapter on Le Nôtre, vol. 2, pp. 57-87.

———. *Les Perrault.* 2 vols. Paris: Perrin, 1926.

Jouin, Henry. *Charles Le Brun et les arts sous Louis XIV.* Paris: Imp. nationale, 1889.

Langlois, Marcel. *Louis XIV et la cour*. Paris: A. Michel, 1926.

Marcel, Pierre. *Charles Le Brun*. Paris: Plon, 1909.

Sainte-Beuve, Charles Augustin. *Portraits of the Seventeenth Century, Historic and Literary*. New York: G. P. Putnam, 1904.

Strachey, Lytton. *Landmarks in French Literature*. New York: Holt, 1912.

Voltaire, François Marie Arouet de. *Le Siècle de Louis XIV*. Paris: E. Belin, 1895.

PHOTOGRAPHIC CREDITS

All photographs were supplied by the author except on the following pages:

Caisse Nationale des Monuments Historiques, Paris   49, 72, 105, 137
Metropolitan Museum of Art, New York   57, 66, 81, 85, 86, 95, 99, 104, 107, 112,
                115, 119, 129, 130, 143, 145, 150, 156
French Government Tourist Office, New York   78, 89, 91, 97
Pierre Auradon, 95 Avenue Mozart, Paris   65, 100, 116, 134, 140

Designed by Ulrich Ruchti